More Praise for *Dare to Serve*

"*Dare to Serve* stands out as one of the most practical, useful books on leadership that I have ever read. Full of real-world examples and grounded in the dramatic turnaround of Popeyes Louisiana Kitchen restaurants, Cheryl shares with us how to serve others with intention, competence, character, courage, and humility. Her practical experience, proven results, and contagious passion to serve others well is an inspiration to all of us who want to make a real difference in the world."

—Bonnie Wurzbacher, Chief Resource Development Officer, World Vision International, and former Senior Vice President, Global Customer Leadership, The Coca-Cola Company

"*Dare to Serve* chronicles both the remarkable turnaround story of Popeyes Louisiana Kitchen, Inc., and Cheryl's inspiring personal journey of discovery, which galvanized her commitment to an unconventional approach to corporate leadership that has yielded remarkable results."

—Andy Stanley, founder, North Point Ministries, Inc.

"*Dare to Serve* offers a candid, behind-the-scenes look at how a struggling restaurant chain was transformed into a soaring brand success through a simple but revolutionary model of leadership based on serving others. This book is a must-read for leaders of all kinds!"

—Phil Cordell, Global Head, Focused Service and Hampton Brand Management, Hilton Worldwide

"Compelling and inspiring! Bachelder makes the case for her people-focused approach to leadership through her real-life experience at Popeyes Louisiana Kitchen. Developed and honed in an industry where service to others is at the very core of what we do, these lessons are sure to translate not only across industries but to our personal lives as well."

—Dawn Sweeney, President and CEO, National Restaurant Association

"Cheryl Bachelder's brave and unconventional approach to the turnaround of Popeyes challenges all of us to step up our game. Cheryl stands in the gap for us, calling us to a purpose that will drive better results for our organizations, while putting the needs of our people and customers ahead of our own."

—Scott MacLellan, CEO, TouchPoint Support Services, a Compass Group company

"By focusing on the purpose-driven success of those she leads, paradoxically, Cheryl Bachelder gets the results we all want from our organizations. *Dare to Serve* is about the gutsy principles she applied to a business desperately in need of a turnaround and the spectacular results she achieved."

—**Tim Irwin, PhD, bestselling author of *Impact***

"This book turned my thinking upside-down. Cheryl shares her road-tested wisdom and shows how and why Dare-to-Serve leadership works so brilliantly. This is a game-changing book and should be required reading for all leaders."

—**Art Barter, President and CEO, Datron Holdings, Inc., and founder and CEO, Servant Leadership Institute**

"*Dare to Serve* is a game changer! The principles outlined create exponential results far beyond what the individual ego will allow. Boards today are looking for Dare-to-Serve type leaders to ignite possibilities in their organizations. This is a must-read for leaders everywhere!"

—**Jane Edison Stevenson, Vice Chairman, Board & CEO Services, Korn Ferry, and coauthor of *Breaking Away***

"Two. That is the number of minutes it took me to realize Cheryl Bachelder is serious about servant leadership, and the number of pages in this book it took to hook me on the importance of her message. *Dare to Serve* will change the way you live and lead—if you dare to let it."

—**Tommy Spaulding, *New York Times* bestselling author of *It's Not Just Who You Know***

DARE
TO SERVE

HOW TO DRIVE SUPERIOR RESULTS
BY SERVING OTHERS

CHERYL BACHELDER

Berrett–Koehler Publishers, Inc.
a BK Business book

Berrett-Koehler Publishers, Inc.
1333 Broadway, Suite 1000
Oakland, CA 94612-1921
Tel: (510) 817-2277   Fax: (510) 817-2278   www.bkconnection.com

Ordering Information

Quantity sales. Special discounts are available on quantity purchases by corporations, associations, and others. For details, contact the "Special Sales Department" at the Berrett-Koehler address above.

Individual sales. Berrett-Koehler publications are available through most bookstores. They can also be ordered directly from Berrett-Koehler: Tel: (800) 929-2929; Fax: (802) 864-7626; www.bkconnection.com

Orders for college textbook/course adoption use. Please contact Berrett-Koehler: Tel: (800) 929-2929; Fax: (802) 864-7626.

Orders by US trade bookstores and wholesalers. Please contact Ingram Publisher Services, Tel: (800) 509-4887; Fax: (800) 838-1149; E-mail: customer.service@ingrampublisherservices .com; or visit www.ingrampublisherservices.com/Ordering for details about electronic ordering.

Popeyes®, Popeyes® Louisiana Kitchen, Inc. and other associated marks are trademarks owned by Popeyes® Louisiana Kitchen, Inc. Other trademarks belong to their respective owners.

Berrett-Koehler and the BK logo are registered trademarks of Berrett-Koehler Publishers, Inc.

Printed in the United States of America

Berrett-Koehler books are printed on long-lasting acid-free paper. When it is available, we choose paper that has been manufactured by environmentally responsible processes. These may include using trees grown in sustainable forests, incorporating recycled paper, minimizing chlorine in bleaching, or recycling the energy produced at the paper mill.

COVER DESIGN Berry Design and Studio Carnelian

PRODUCED BY WILSTED & TAYLOR PUBLISHING SERVICES
Copy editing: Nancy Evans   Design and composition: Nancy Koerner

Library of Congress Cataloging-in-Publication Data

Bachelder, Cheryl.
    Dare to serve : how to drive superior results by serving others / Cheryl Bachelder. — First edition.
        pages cm
    Includes bibliographical references and index.
    ISBN 978-1-62656-235-6 (hardcover)
    1. Leadership.   2. Servant leadership.   3. Organizational effectiveness.   I. Title.
    HD57.7.B322 2015
    658.4′092—dc23   2014044655

ISBN: 978-1-62656-235-6
Popeyes Special Edition ISBN: 978-1-62656-593-7

First Edition
20 19 18 17 16 15   10 9 8 7 6 5 4 3 2 1

To my grandparents,
*   Jack and Bertha, John and Gertrude;*
to my parents, Max and Marge;
to my siblings, Beth, Laura, and David
*   and their spouses;*
to my husband, Chris, and daughters,
*   Tracy, Kathleen, and Katerina;*
to sons-in-law and grandchildren,
*   current and future—*
because of you I know the joy of love,
*   family, and faith.*

To the Popeyes Leadership Team with whom
I have served—I am deeply grateful for your
competence, your character, and your service.

To the entire Popeyes family for making
this story possible—it has been amazing
to be on this journey with you.

All glory be to God the Father,
for He sent His Son who dared to serve us all.

Contents

THE **DARE-TO-SERVE** LEADER

AT THE BEGINNING OF A BROADWAY SHOW, the lights dim, the music plays, and the audience waits for the spotlight to hit the stage. When the main actor appears, the story begins.

So it is with leadership. When you become a leader, people wait for you to step into the spotlight on center stage. All eyes are fixed on you—waiting to see who you are, what you will say, and what you will do. After all, you are the leader.

What if the spotlight appeared on stage, and you were not in it? What would happen then?

The people would be confused. They would wonder where you were. They would think that you didn't understand your role.

Until they realized what you were doing.

You are a different kind of leader. Not seeking the spotlight.

In fact, you have walked off the stage to find the light crew.

You will shift the focus of the spotlight—to the people you have been asked to lead.

You will lead the people to daring destinations—far beyond their imagination.

You will focus intensely on serving them well on the journey.

You will help them discover meaning in their work and principles in their actions.

You will dare to serve.

THE SPOTLIGHT PROBLEM

Conventional leadership thinking puts the leader in the spotlight.

Conventional leaders assume the power position and declare a new vision. Grabbing the spotlight, these leaders have all the answers. They are high achievers, though perhaps a bit self-absorbed. We tolerate that, because they are going places that we want to go. If they are successful, we will be successful. So we think.

At the other extreme, we think of humble servant leaders. They shun the spotlight. They listen carefully to the people. They involve the people in decisions. They make decisions that serve the people well; they give others credit. We wonder about these leaders. We like them, but we fear they will not get us to success. Could they deliver superior performance results? We doubt it.

We conclude that it is the leader *in the spotlight* who delivers results. Because, of course, "nice guys finish last."

Have you worked for a leader who loves the spotlight? Were *you* served well?

My message is simple, but unconventional. If you move yourself out of the spotlight and dare to serve others, you will deliver superior performance results.

Most haven't heard this before. Many will be skeptical, even confused.

What about you?

Perhaps you think selfless service is for charitable causes and saints. Perhaps you think serving is weak and cowardly, not bold and courageous. Perhaps you think, "I've never met this kind of leader and doubt that they exist."

It's time to reconsider your assumptions.

This is a different kind of leader with a rare combination of traits, *courageous* enough to take the people to a daring destination, yet *humble* enough to selflessly serve others on the journey. The dynamic tension between daring and serving creates the conditions for superior performance.

This is a Dare-to-Serve Leader.

THE DISCOVERY

There's nothing fundamentally wrong with our country except that the leaders of all our major organizations are operating on the wrong assumptions.

ROBERT TOWNSEND, *UP THE ORGANIZATION*

About fifteen years ago, I began to study leadership with a newfound intensity. At the time, I had been working for large public companies for twenty years. I had been promoted numerous times and had worked for a wide range of people: some great leaders and some terrible leaders.

I started looking at the traits of the leaders I had loved— the ones whom I had worked the hardest for—the ones who had brought out my best performance. I discovered that the leaders I admired most not only were great to work for but also led their teams to remarkable results.

What kind of leader would I aspire to become? What model would I follow?

In my leadership journey, I have uncovered something that, in your heart of hearts, you already know.

Your favorite leaders have been decidedly different. Their motives go beyond self-interest. They challenge you to pursue daring, bold aspirations that create an exciting place to work. They shun the spotlight in favor of serving a higher purpose. They evidence principles in their daily decisions. You not only love these leaders but also perform your very best work for them.

So now the question is, what kind of leader will YOU choose to be? Will you dare to serve?

THIS BOOK IS FOR YOU

This book is for practitioners—people leading right now —in any organization, large or small, at any level. If you have been given a position to lead people, this book is for you.

The inspiration for this book is not a group of famous leaders, CEOs, or celebrities, but ordinary people who want to do extraordinary things wherever they are given the opportunity to lead—at work, at home, or in the community. I am privileged to meet these inspirational people daily in my work with the people who lead Popeyes restaurants—from New Orleans, Louisiana, to Singapore. Restaurant leaders dare to serve far more often than the CEOs I have met. They have inspired me to tell this story.

WHAT WILL YOU LEARN?

This book brings together the discoveries of my leadership journey in the hope that this perspective can help you become a Dare-to-Serve Leader with superior performance results. What I propose is not an impossible dream, but it is unconventional thinking.

The first half of the book is the story of the turnaround of Popeyes Louisiana Kitchen, Inc., a publicly traded global restaurant chain I am honored to lead. The Popeyes story provides a real-world example of how one leadership team dared to serve the people well—and produced industry-leading results.

The second half of the book is about how you can become a Dare-to-Serve Leader. It offers thoughts and reflections to guide you in becoming the most effective leader you can be.

What is the most difficult thing I will suggest to you?

You will have to take yourself out of the spotlight.

The curtain will open, the lights will dim, and the people will be waiting.

You will not do the expected. You will not step into the spotlight.

Instead, you will find a way to get that spotlight to shine on others. You will help them pursue dreams and find meaning in work. You will grow their capabilities. You will model principles in daily decisions that build an environment of trust and commitment. When the people figure out what you are doing, they will find that you are a leader they want to follow on a path to the best performance results of their life.

If you become a Dare-to-Serve Leader, your legacy will be your impact on the lives of the people you lead and the outstanding results you created together.

WHERE DID I GET THIS IDEA?

A dozen years ago, I met Jim Collins, the author of *Good to Great*, at a meeting of Yum! Brands leaders. He presented the findings of his book, describing a new type of top-performing leader: a Level V Leader. He said that Level V Leaders are a "paradoxical mix of personal humility and professional will. They are ambitious, to be sure, but ambitious first and foremost for the company, not themselves."

Collins's work established a case for servant leadership called by another name, the Level V Leader. It included financial data proving that Level V leaders delivered superior performance results.

The idea fascinated me.

I wondered, "Is it possible to be humble and ambitious? What would it mean to put the people and the enterprise first—above self-interest? How would this inspire superior performance?"

Collins's book sold more than 2.5 million copies. But will these findings change your approach to leadership?

THE OPPORTUNITY ARRIVES . . .

In 2007, I got my chance to test Dare-to-Serve Leadership in a real-world setting with seven talented people, collectively called the Popeyes Leadership Team.

We made a daring decision to serve others well by pursuing a bold ambition for the enterprise. We then established a purpose and a set of principles to govern our leadership.

We wanted to prove that we could drive superior performance results by leading as the handful of humble, serving leaders we read about in books like *Leadership Is an Art, The Soul of the Firm,* and *Firms of Endearment* had done.

At the time, Popeyes was a struggling restaurant chain with a long history of declining sales and profits. It offered a classic "turnaround" opportunity. Leadership had been a revolving door of short-lived CEOs—four in seven years.

In those same seven years, guest traffic had declined. Same-store sales were negative. Restaurant average unit volume and profitability had fallen to dangerously low levels. New restaurant returns were anemic. The relationship between the company and its franchisees was on the rocks. As for investors, the stock price had slid from a peak of $34 per share in 2002 to $13 on the day I joined the company.

What better time for a grand experiment in leadership? What if we were able to prove that a daring aspiration and selfless service to others could deliver superior performance results? What if a purpose and a set of principles could guide us to industry-leading performance? What if we did this under the scrutiny of a public-company environment, garnering the attention of those cynical, short-term Wall Street investors?

Fast-forward to today. Popeyes restaurants have experienced six years of growth. Average restaurant sales have climbed by 25 percent. Market share has grown from 14 to 21 percent. The profitability of Popeyes restaurants has improved 40 percent in terms of real dollars, with restaurant profit margins up from 18 to 22 percent.

The franchisees who own our restaurants are so delighted with the business results that they have rapidly remodeled existing restaurants and are feverishly building new Popeyes that are providing excellent returns on their investment.

The stock price is now in the $40 range—up 450 percent in six years.

The company is now the darling of the industry . . . a favorite of the franchisees . . . a favorite of lenders . . . a favorite of investors . . . and a case study in serving up superior performance results.

The secret to Popeyes turnaround performance?

We dared to serve.

HOW TO GET THE MOST FROM THIS BOOK

As I grew up, I learned many of my leadership lessons from my father. Daddy Max, as I called him, served as vice president of National Semiconductor Corporation for many years, primarily overseeing manufacturing operations in Asia.

My dad was an accomplished and perceptive storyteller, and most of his stories were about how to lead people. Over dinner he would talk about his day at work. Always included in his story was the "moral of the story" to make sure we understood the underlying leadership lesson.

One evening my dad was pacing the kitchen floor, visibly upset. When I asked him what was bothering him, he told me that tomorrow he would be laying off people at the manufacturing plant. He told me he was sick over it. People he cared about would be unemployed. Families would suffer from the loss. Moral of the story: letting people go should make your stomach turn—never take it lightly.

My dad and mom raised four children, each of whom became a CEO or president of a company, in four different industries. The leadership lessons in those dinnertable stories served us well.

Similarly, I will share leadership stories—what I have observed, reflected on, and learned. I encourage you to seek the "moral of the story," to discover the leadership lesson. Throughout these chapters, you will find Dare-to-Serve Reflections to help you think about the leadership role you are in today and the best way to influence and steward the people entrusted to your care. In this process, you will consider whether you want to be a Dare-to-Serve Leader.

The world is waiting for leaders to come forward who can steward an organization's people and resources to superior performance. When you choose to humbly serve others and courageously lead them to daring destinations, the team will give you their very best performance. And the spotlight will be found shining on the remarkable results of the organization as a whole.

May you be inspired to be a Dare-to-Serve Leader who drives superior results. And may you spend the rest of your days teaching others to do the same.

Cheryl A. Bachelder
Chief Executive Officer
Popeyes Louisiana Kitchen, Inc.

PART ONE

HOW TO DRIVE
SUPERIOR RESULTS

I have not always enjoyed success as a leader.
In the fall of 2003, unable to sustain a turnaround of KFC restaurants, my boss suggested that it was time for me to leave. In other words, I got fired.

Few things are as clarifying as losing your job. My confidence was shaken. This was supposed to be the pinnacle position of my career—my day in the spotlight.

Perhaps that was the problem. The spotlight was not where I was supposed to be.

After meandering through a few consulting projects, I decided that my "retirement" work would be serving on boards. I was honored to join the boards of True Value Hardware Company and AFC Enterprises, Inc., the parent company of Popeyes.

In the spring of 2007, the CEO of Popeyes left the company. After a search committee reviewed several candidates to be the next CEO, the board asked me to lead the organization.

Looking back, this move was providential. In my previous role as a leader, I had been humbled. Now

I would be given a chance to redeem that experience by leading the people of Popeyes.

I had a chance to step out of the spotlight; to lead the people to a daring destination; to serve them well along the journey; and to create the conditions for superior performance.

Popeyes' performance results have been remarkable. I only wish I had been humbled sooner.

ONE

WHOM WILL WE SERVE?

*It begins with the natural feeling
that one wants to serve, to serve first.*

ROBERT K. GREENLEAF,
THE SERVANT AS LEADER

I AM AN ETERNAL OPTIMIST, a certified member of the positive-thinking club.

When we were growing up, my mother woke my siblings and me by playing loud music on the stereo and saying "Good morning! It's a beautiful day. Rise and shine." There was no opportunity for negativity. It was *going* to be a good day.

I continued this tradition with my children. The mantra of their childhood was, "Your attitude is your altitude." They still grimace when I say it, but the message is etched in their minds. Decide how you will approach this day—and that will determine your day.

The same is true in leadership—*your attitude is your altitude.*

When I joined Popeyes, the place needed an attitude adjustment. The problem? The people we were responsible for leading were viewed as "a pain in the neck."

The franchise owners were "difficult." The restaurant teams were "poor performers." The guests were "impossible to please." The board members were "challenging." The investors were "not on our side."

The first step in turning around your organization's performance? Think positively about the people you lead. Your attitude will determine the altitude of your performance results.

DARE-TO-SERVE REFLECTION #1 *How do you think about the people you lead? Are they a "pain in the neck" or essential to the future success of the organization?*

THE BUSINESS SITUATION

Popeyes' performance in 2007 couldn't have been much worse. Every data point that we measured was going the wrong way. Sales were declining. Guest satisfaction was worst-in-class. Restaurant profits were down in absolute dollars and margin. Morale at the company was negative. Franchise owners were mad and "sick and tired" of bad results. Investors were disappointed in the stock performance and wanted answers. The board was tired of hearing promises that did not materialize.

In the following year, economic conditions would deteriorate as well. Lehman Brothers would disappear. The stock market would fall precipitously. The United States would head into a steep recession that contributed to the slowdown of the global economy. Times were not good.

The odds were stacked against a successful Popeyes turnaround.

What leadership approach would lead to success?

NOT LIKE THEM

Picture eight members of the Popeyes Leadership Team stuffed in a small conference room at an Atlanta facility called the Buckhead Club. Our job for the day? To make a conscious decision on how we would lead Popeyes to sustained success.

We started by making lists of the traits we admired in the best leaders of our careers. Interestingly, the conversation quickly turned to the traits that we wanted to avoid, traits that characterized the worst leaders we had met.

On the flip chart, we listed words like *self-absorbed*, *arrogant*, and *condescending*.

Before we knew it, we were telling stories to one another about the difficult people we had worked for. It became a "can you top this?" contest.

That was a turning point in our leadership of Popeyes.

Our first decision—we did not want to lead like "them."

We started talking about our favorite leadership philosophies. One person mentioned a book that had been influential in his life, *Leadership Is an Art* by Max De Pree. Published in 1989 by the then-CEO of Herman Miller, the book put forth a novel idea—that leaders are *stewards* of the people and the organizations they lead. When leaders create environments where followers thrive, the business performs well.

Others brought up books that they liked—authored by Patrick Lencioni, Stephen Covey, Jim Collins, and more—and a theme emerged in the conversation. We wanted to be leaders who *served well* the people, brand, and organization we had been given. We didn't want to fall prey to the self-focused leadership style we had observed in others. Our belief was that serving people well would generate better business results.

One member of the team said, "I think there is a name for this kind of leadership. Give me a minute to do a web search." He was the only one with an iPhone at the time and he quickly came up with the answer. A man named Robert Greenleaf had written about a leadership approach called *servant leadership*. It was about serving the people well—above self-interest.

That's it!

Serving others over self.

We quickly agreed that this servant leadership notion would guide us going forward.

DARE-TO-SERVE REFLECTION #2 *Think about difficult leaders you have worked for. Have you made a conscious decision to lead differently than "them"?*

But there was one more thing. We believed that servant leadership would deliver superior results. The performance of the enterprise would be the evidence that we had served others well.

Before leaving the conference room that day, we had

a draft of the Popeyes purpose and principles that would guide our leadership for years to come.

Our purpose: To inspire servant leaders to achieve superior results.

Our principles: Six behaviors we saw as essential to serving the people well *and* delivering superior performance—passion, listening, planning, coaching, accountability, and humility.

We made a decision that day: we decided to serve.

Dare-to-Serve Leaders begin by intentionally deciding on their attitude and leadership approach.

- Decide to think positively about the people you lead.

- Decide to be a leader who serves others over self-interest.

It is both courageous and humbling to remove yourself from the spotlight and shift your focus and energy toward serving others well. This is how you create an environment for superior results.

THE MANY CHOICES

If we were going to serve people well at Popeyes—*whom* would we serve?

We listed all the possibilities on the conference room flip chart: the guests; the shareholders; the franchise owners; the team members; the board of directors; the regulators; the accountants. Had we missed anyone?

Someone said, "Don't we have to serve all of those people?"

Hmmm. Could be true. Let's go through each possibility.

In restaurants, the ultimate goal is to serve your restaurant guest well. After all, guests buy the food—without them, there is no business. If they are not served well, they don't come back.

We are a public company. Shareholders have invested in this business and expect a reasonable, preferably good, return on that investment. We are hired as their "stewards." Without their investment, we will not be funded for growth. If they are not well served, they exit our stock—and the stock price falls—reducing our access to capital and the value of the enterprise.

Popeyes licenses the rights to use the brand and the operating system to franchise owners. These owners borrow money and invest it in building Popeyes restaurants, hiring and training restaurant crews, and building relationships with the communities and guests we serve. Without franchisees, we do not have a global restaurant chain— they drive our expansion. If they are not well served, they exit the brand—selling or closing restaurants—and reduce our ability to serve guests our famous Louisiana recipes.

DARE-TO-SERVE REFLECTION #3 *Who are the most important people you serve—the owner, the boss, the customer, the employees? Which one is your primary focus?*

It takes about 60,000 team members to run our more than 2,200 restaurants around the globe. These team members get up every day, come to work, prepare the food, serve the guests, clean up the place, and close the doors. These team members feed and serve our guests.

If we do not serve the team members well, they go to work somewhere else. Without them, we are not open for business.

In our business, we have many choices of people to serve; they are all important. Would we serve them equally, or would we pick one as our primary focus?

THE CHOICE WE MADE

At Popeyes, we chose to serve the franchise owners well as our first priority.

In franchising, we make money in two basic ways: we collect royalties on restaurant sales and we collect franchise fees when a new restaurant is built. Those monies fund the infrastructure of the company so we can carry out the service obligations of our franchise contract: brand marketing, new product innovation, operating systems, quality assurance, and more.

We have long-term contracts with our franchise owners—typically twenty-year agreements with options to renew. Thus, we have long-term relationships with the owners who borrowed the money to build our restaurants and hire the people who serve our guests. Franchise owners do the heavy lifting.

As we looked at our options for whom we would serve, we thought the franchise owners merited our immediate attention. They had made sizable investments and were committed by contract to operate our brand. If they did not prosper, there was no chance Popeyes sales would go up (royalties) or franchise fees would increase (new openings). Either franchise owners would succeed or Popeyes would fail.

This decision is not typical in our industry. Franchisors

and franchisees are constantly in conflict—arguing about the contract, the business strategy, the restaurant design, the promotion pricing, or the cost of the food. If the conflict gets particularly bad, threats of lawsuits quickly surface.

When I joined Domino's Pizza in 1995, Domino's franchisees sued the company in a class-action lawsuit. When I joined KFC in February 2001, I learned of the long history of conflict between KFC franchisees and the franchisor, with a negotiated settlement in 1996. In my restaurant career, the media has reported on troubled franchisee/franchisor relationships at well-known brands such as Burger King and Quiznos, among others.

Interestingly, unresolved conflict with franchise owners never leads to operational excellence or superior sales and profit performance. Instead, franchise systems with high internal conflict have negative business results. It is predictable. Nonetheless, franchisees and franchisors typically don't get along.

So we asked ourselves a few questions.

What if we dared to be different from our peers? What if we dared to serve the franchise owners well?

What would that look like?

We would have to work closely with the franchisees to choose the vital few initiatives that would improve performance. Once we were aligned on the right plan, the franchise owners would implement that plan in the restaurants. When the plan was executed well by the restaurants, performance results would improve. When sales and profits improved, franchisees would build more restaurants. New restaurant growth would create value for the shareholders.

This could work.

Our success would begin and end with the success of the Popeyes franchise owners.

LOVING THOSE YOU LEAD

Here's a tough question. Do you love the people you've decided to serve?

It helps.

One Popeyes leader says it this way: "If you are in the franchising business, you should love the franchisees."

To love franchisees, you have to love entrepreneurs. Entrepreneurs are passionate. They take risks. They invest for the future. They are ambitious. They are definitely not corporate bureaucrats. They do not have much patience with people holding MBA degrees or offering up expensive harebrained ideas. What if the most important people in your business are entrepreneurs? You must decide to love them.

As a side note, I can't imagine why someone wouldn't love franchise owners. I'm biased by my worldview. I believe that democratic capitalism creates conditions for entrepreneurs to invest and grow small businesses. The entrepreneurs are pursuing a dream, and owning a small business is their path to that dream. In the United States, we call this the "American Dream." People come to this country just for the chance to build their own business.

These are the people we are honored to serve at Popeyes. The Popeyes franchise owners decided to take the risk and invest sweat-equity and financial capital into building and operating Popeyes restaurants. They are amazing people with equally amazing life stories.

Here are just a few examples of the many franchise owners in our system whom I love.

Lal Sultanzada is a Popeyes franchisee in New York City. Lal immigrated to this country from Afghanistan. His first job was working in a chicken restaurant in Harlem. Eventually he saved enough money to buy that restaurant and he became a Popeyes franchise owner. Today, Lal has dozens of restaurants operating to the highest of standards. His restaurant leaders win many Popeyes awards. I love that Lal is now sending his children to college to follow in his footsteps and run this highly successful family restaurant business.

Mack Wilbourn operates three Popeyes restaurants at the Hartsfield-Jackson Atlanta International Airport. Two of them have the largest sales volume in our system. Mack hires people who take fabulous care of the guests. You will often hear the restaurant manager, Edith, say, "Honey, you are looking good today—what can I get you for dinner?" I love the warmth and positive energy that Mack's teams bring to our guests. They set the standard for service excellence.

John Broderson is a Popeyes franchisee who owns urban restaurants in Milwaukee, Chicago, Detroit, and Puerto Rico. His career began working in a troubled Popeyes restaurant in Chicago that his father had purchased. Over time, John developed a talented team of restaurant leaders who routinely win awards in our system. Recently John went back to Chicago to seek out that first Popeyes restaurant he worked in—and he bought it. I love the fact that John invests in urban neighborhoods, providing career opportunities to many.

Harry Stafford invested in the restaurant business after

a successful career in law and Texas oil. Today his organization owns and operates more than a dozen Popeyes restaurants with excellence. At the age of seventy-five, Harry remains one of our most forward-looking entrepreneurs, buying property and expanding his Popeyes network in the Houston area. I love that Harry leads with integrity and has invested his time serving as a leader in the Popeyes system, chairing a new committee each year.

Amin Dhanani is the sixth son of a family that immigrated to the United States to be entrepreneurs. Today his family is one of the largest operators of Burger King restaurants as well as Popeyes. This owner is one of the boldest and fastest-expanding operators in our system, owning and operating Popeyes in multiple states. I love Amin's daring aspiration for expanding Popeyes across the nation as fast as possible.

Guillermo Perales owns Popeyes restaurants in Oklahoma, Texas, and Florida. Beyond Popeyes, he is the largest Hispanic franchisee in America, owning multiple retail businesses. When Guillermo saw the turnaround of Popeyes performance results, he decided to become one of our fastest-growing developers. I love that he is willing to invest in Popeyes' future.

Danny Gililland operates Popeyes in Little Rock, Arkansas. Danny loves restaurant operating systems and his wife, Lynda, loves training restaurant teams. The Gilillands volunteer to test just about every piece of restaurant equipment or new training process that our team comes up with. I love that Danny and Lynda never get tired of debugging these inventions, and their enthusiastic efforts have helped us make better decisions for our system.

Nareg Amirian is a second-generation Popeyes franchisee, following his successful father, Bobken Amirian, an Armenian who emigrated from Iran. Nareg combines his experience in the family business with an MBA from the UCLA Anderson School of Management and runs restaurants in Las Vegas and Los Angeles. I love that Nareg has courageously stepped forward to run the family business for the next generation.

Now I have to pause and apologize to every Popeyes franchisee whom I did not mention. Please know that I love you, too!

DARE-TO-SERVE REFLECTION #4 *What are the specific qualities you love in the people you lead?*

We have more than three hundred franchise owners at Popeyes—and I love them all. These are hardworking people who have taken bold risks to grow Popeyes and to serve our guests well. They are inspiring people, people to be admired. They deserve to be loved. They deserve to be served.

THE DIFFICULTY OF SERVING

If you choose to be a Dare-to-Serve Leader, you'll have one very big obstacle to overcome.

Yourself.

It is easy to say that you want to serve others well, but much harder to do so in daily life.

This topic is seldom discussed out in the open. It would not be seen as admirable to admit that your leadership approach is aimed at serving *yourself* well. In fact, I've never heard anyone actually say this out loud.

Interestingly, I have heard many *followers* tell me that their leader was self-absorbed. It turns out that the people know your motive, whether *you* know it or not.

They know if you are making a decision to make yourself look good. They know if you are angling to get promoted. They know if you are hoping for a raise to buy a new house. They know your motives by your actions, not your words.

No one is unscathed by this truth. I am as guilty as anyone else. And you?

WHAT'S IN IT FOR YOU?

Even leaders who say they want to be Dare-to-Serve Leaders have this question in their own head—what's in it for me? How will I benefit?

You're not a bad person for considering this question. You're just like everybody else, you think of yourself first. So let's tackle this question before going further.

Here are the five benefits to you of becoming a Dare-to-Serve Leader.

Benefit to You No. 1 *People will tell you the stuff you need to know.* Self-centered leaders don't invest time in getting to know their people. When the people don't know you well, they won't tell you what is going on in the organization. You miss out on mission-critical facts that you need to make decisions. Serving the people well requires that you spend time knowing the people well.

Benefit to You No. 2 *People will be more likely to follow your bold vision.* As the leader, you are expected to create the vision for the organization. No one will debate that. But you don't actually implement the vision; you need followers who believe in your vision and are motivated to do the work. To be highly motivated, the people need to know that you have their best interests at heart. Serving the people well requires that you take their interests into account as you lead the organization.

Benefit to You No. 3 *People will actually do the stuff you need to get done without a lot of reminding.* Self-centered leaders who insist on making all the decisions make the people "leader dependent." Unable to perform on their own, the followers wait for the leader to tell them what to do. They do the minimum, unless you follow up repeatedly. Serving the people well requires that you empower the team, let them make decisions, and let them lead.

Benefit to You No. 4 *People will perform better.* Self-centered leaders create anxious, unsafe work environments where there is no benefit seen for taking risks or growing in capability. The environment is governed by threats and fear; a scarcity mentality prevails. When work is all about the leader's own ambitions, there is no good reason to give your best performance. In contrast, if you serve the people well, you will provide a safe environment focused on personal growth, promotion opportunities, and the fun of "winning" together. This leads to winning results.

Benefit to You No. 5 *People will watch out for you and protect you from yourself.* Self-centered leaders create the conditions for a lapse in personal integrity. The leader who receives little feedback from the team becomes overconfident, without checks and balances. The leader's compass becomes "do the right thing, as long as it advances my career." This blind spot causes the leader to miss the truly moral decisions that are right for the people and the enterprise, regardless of cost to self. The leader who serves the people well finds that the people protect you from yourself; they have your back.

WHAT MINDSET TRAPS LIE AHEAD?

If you and your team commit to becoming Dare-to-Serve Leaders, certain mindsets will trip you up on a regular basis. Here are just a few of the mindset traps our team has experienced at Popeyes.

Mindset Trap No. 1: "But I am right." It is difficult to stay in a mindset of serving others when they do not agree with you. Your first inclination is to think, "But I am right, and they are wrong."

In leadership, and certainly in the franchising business, this happens often—we disagree with one another—but we must work together to move the business forward. We have found that acting in unison as a restaurant chain always works better than acting in disunity. Nonetheless, it is frustrating when we fail to gain alignment with our franchise owners, particularly when the facts are on our side. Our impatient "self" wishes we could make the decision "solo." While that might be efficient, it is does not serve franchise owners well.

In the seven years we have led Popeyes, this situation has occurred multiple times. We recommended a business plan that probably was sound and probably would have worked just fine. Our franchise owners did not agree. We slowed down, swallowed our pride, and prioritized the *relationship* with our franchise owners over being right. We may have lost some momentum in the short term, but we gained alignment that led to a well-executed plan in the marketplace. Sometimes you must go slow to go fast.

Mindset Trap No. 2: "What's wrong with these followers?" One of the big challenges of leadership is getting the followers to go with you on the journey. This can be exhausting—a constant need to persuade and re-persuade the followers. It makes you wonder: Why don't they see the bold vision? Why don't they see the opportunities ahead?

Persuading more than three hundred Popeyes franchise owners to agree on a decision can be exhausting work, and when it's not going well your self-talk begins to say, "What is wrong with these people?" Our franchising contract gives our company the right to make certain decisions—we could simply say, "It's in the contract."

That is tempting, but it is not serving. We remind ourselves that influencing and persuading others is ultimately more effective than exercising authority over them. At Popeyes, we have a contract if we need it—but we want to use it only as a last resort.

One tactic we have used effectively to manage ourselves in this circumstance is this—when one of our senior leaders gets "exhausted" with the process of bringing the franchisees into agreement with us, we let someone else take over who is fresh and more objective about the matter. This gives the one leader a rest and a chance to recover positive energy, while the pinch hitter leads the decision to closure.

Our franchisees have come to appreciate this behavior of the team. It gives them confidence that someone will always stay in the room with them to hear their input, even when one of us gets tired of the topic. In fact, today, after seven years of practice, our franchisees will often request that another leader get involved in a matter if there is difficulty getting to alignment.

Mindset Trap No. 3: "We wish they trusted us." Everyone knows that trust is essential to high-performing teams, but it isn't easy to attain. Once you get to trust, it can disappear in a moment's time. Why is this trust thing so difficult?

Stephen Covey taught that human beings have emotional bank accounts: if you make positive deposits over time, trust builds in the relationship. If you make negative withdrawals over time, trust erodes.

At the outset, we believed this to be true in the franchising business. Our leadership team invested in making lots of positive deposits in the trust bank account of our owners. We envisioned that each shared "win" would be a deposit that would build a high-trust partnership. Arguably, the performance results of the company alone should have built immense trust with our franchise owners.

Yet we've discovered that trust does not accumulate between a franchisor and a franchisee. Trust is built for one decision, but seldom carries forward to the next one.

At first we were discouraged by this learning—it seemed unfair and unreasonable. Our franchisees constantly remind us of the decisions of the past that have broken trust—there are many in a forty-three-year company history. Those memories are elephant-sized and they won't go away.

Bemoaning this lack of deserved trust is a self-serving mindset. Instead, we encourage one another to "be the adult." Another way to say this—we model what trust looks like and behave accordingly. The Popeyes Leadership Team has strong emotional bank accounts with one another, and that provides the high trust work environment we need to be effective leaders.

I've come to understand the similarity between working with franchise owners and parenting an adopted child. Because of a history of distrust in their early life, they may never trust you—but you can still lead them, love them, and serve them well.

WHOM WILL WE SERVE?—THE PERFORMANCE RESULTS

To measure how well we have kept our promise to serve our franchise owners, we have conducted a survey every summer to get feedback from them. This is our report card on how we serve our most important customer.

The table below shows how we have performed on the key metrics over a five-year period.

Popeyes franchise-owner satisfaction ratings have improved dramatically over the last five years. Each year the

Popeyes Franchise Owner Survey Results

Percent of franchisees rating Popeyes good, very good, or excellent

	2008	2013	Change
How would you rate the overall quality of the Popeyes system?	66	95	+29
Would you invest in Popeyes again?	76	93	+17
Would you recommend Popeyes to another potential franchisee?	67	90	+23
Popeyes is committed to a positive, long-term relationship with me.	66	91	+25
Popeyes understands that if I am successful, they are successful.	76	91	+15

survey provides us with insight into areas of opportunity for future improvements. This is part of how we maintain our commitment to serve the franchisees well.

DARE-TO-SERVE REFLECTION #5 *How do you gain meaningful feedback from those you serve?*

THE DECISION TO SERVE

The first decision of a Dare-to-Serve Leader? You decide to serve the people well.

This decision has many benefits—perhaps the most important is this: People who are well served are more likely to give their best to the organization. That gives you the best prospect of getting superior performance results.

Consciously decide whom you will serve.

Don't leave this to chance.

At the outset, I suggest that you focus on serving one specific group of people. You will be more intentional in your decisions to serve them well. You will be more likely to notice the challenges of serving and make adjustments in your approach. You will be more likely to experience the benefits of superior performance.

At Popeyes, we discovered the performance power of serving others by focusing first on our franchise owners. This success has given us conviction about the importance of serving every constituent in our company well—the restaurant manager, the employee, the guest, the vendor partner, the investor, the board.

Dare-to-Serve Leadership is a *mindset* for approaching every constituent.

Bring your team together today—and decide to serve.

TWO

WHAT IS THE **DARING** DESTINATION?

The bravest are the tenderest,—
the loving are the daring.

BAYARD JOSEPH TAYLOR (1825–1878)

AROUND THE DINNER TABLE, our family likes to discuss words. This habit comes from my husband of more than thirty years. He cares deeply about the proper use of words. Recently in one of these evening discussions, we contemplated the meaning of the terms *paradox* and *oxymoron.*

The word *paradox*, as defined by Merriam-Webster, means "something . . . that is made up of two opposite things and that seems impossible but is actually true or possible." The word originates from the Greek word *paradoxon*, meaning "contrary to expectation."

An *oxymoron* is considered a "compressed paradox." In terms I can understand, that means two words used together that are seemingly contradictory, such as "silent alarm." The origin of *oxymoron* is also Greek—a combination of two Greek words, *oxys* meaning sharp or keen, and *moros* meaning foolish. Sharp and foolish? It turns out that even the word *oxymoron* is an oxymoron.

So to make this dinner game more interesting, we shared our favorite oxymorons:

Live recording

Mandatory option

Jumbo shrimp

Paid volunteer

Minor crisis

To keep my head in the game, I start thinking about business . . .

Assistant supervisor

Friendly takeover

Limited guarantee

Working vacation

Then my mind wanders to leadership:

Daring Serving

Seemingly contradictory—an oxymoron?

NO DARING DESTINATION

At the beginning of this Popeyes turnaround, there was no clearly stated destination for the people and the enterprise. The people were committed and hardworking, but they did not know where they were going. When you asked people where the organization would be in five years, they responded with either "I don't know" or "I wish I knew."

Popeyes wasn't winning any games. The team was discouraged, even exasperated. They were struggling with no evidence of a turnaround in sight. They needed to know what tournament they were playing in. How else would they know how to prepare for a game? How would they recognize a win?

Popeyes needed a daring destination—for the people and the enterprise. What bold goals would mobilize the Popeyes team to high performance? How would we bring a daring aspiration to life for the organization?

A Dare-to-Serve Leader pursues a daring destination for the people and the enterprise. You can't serve the people well if you don't have aspirations for the team to be wildly successful. The steps:

- State the daring destination with a plausible business case.

- Focus on the vital few actions, the hard things that must be addressed.

- Commit the resources needed to reach the destination, as evidence of your conviction.

- Create a work environment that brings out the best in people and performance.

- Have the courage to measure and report progress.

PROVIDING A DARING DESTINATION

> *"Would you tell me, please, which way I ought to go from here?"*
> *"That depends a good deal on where you want to get to,"*
>   *said the Cat.*
> *"I don't much care where," said Alice.*
> *"Then it doesn't matter which way you go," said the Cat.*
>   LEWIS CARROLL,
>   *ALICE'S ADVENTURES IN WONDERLAND*

The first time I met the Popeyes franchisees was at the Popeyes International Franchise Conference in Orlando, Florida—a gathering of the franchise owners and their management teams with the Popeyes leaders who support them. My first day on the job involved standing on a huge stage in front of the business owners with a teleprompter and a PowerPoint presentation.

Looking back, I probably should have worn a bulletproof vest. With my optimistic personality, I told the franchise owners how thrilled I was to join Popeyes. I shared a few of the reasons why I thought we had a great opportunity in front of us. The most important thing I established that day was a picture of the future—a daring destination we could aspire to reach together.

The vision I shared was this:

One day Popeyes will again be the hottest concept among U.S. quick-service restaurants. We will have average unit volumes of $1.2 million. We will have quick drive-thrus that delight our guests. The franchise owners will be making 22 percent restaurant operating profit. And we will build more restaurants with good financial returns to the franchise owners. Over time, we will more than double the size of this chain.

Our aspirations for Popeyes were conveyed in a four-part plan—we called it the Roadmap to Results. The four pillars of the plan were: build a distinctive brand, run great restaurants, grow restaurant profits, and accelerate quality openings. The Roadmap wasn't rocket science—or wildly different from our competitors' plans—but the words clearly explained what we were going to do to become a growing, prosperous restaurant chain.

We defined the future state of Popeyes. Nobody had any reason to believe we were actually going to reach those goals. Nonetheless, the franchise owners were temporarily calmed by the idea that we *had* bold goals and a vision of future success.

DARE-TO-SERVE REFLECTION #6 *What daring destination have you established for your team and organization? What strategies will ensure the team reaches the destination?*

A friend of mine says that when you lead a team it is like taking your family on vacation. Until the family knows where they are going, they won't know whether to bring their winter coats or their bathing suits.

Define the destination so that the team can pack their suitcase.

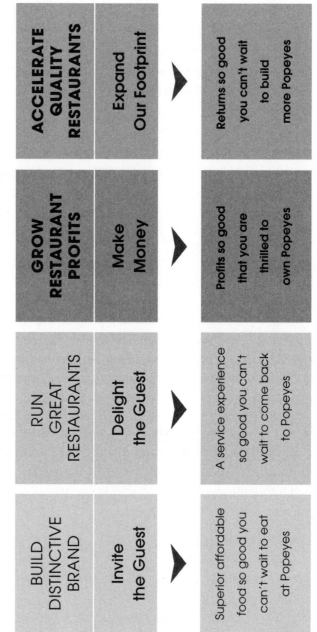

FOCUS ON THE VITAL FEW

People think focus means saying yes *to the thing you've got to focus on. But that's not what it means at all. It means saying* no *to the hundred other good ideas that there are. You have to pick carefully. I'm actually as proud of the things we haven't done as the things I have done.*

STEVE JOBS, APPLE WORLDWIDE DEVELOPERS
CONFERENCE, MAY 13–16, 1997

After the first big global conference with franchisees, the Popeyes Leadership Team went back to the Atlanta headquarters and held our first meeting together. We were the team that was going to figure out *how* to get to the daring destination we had declared at the franchise meeting. In other words, we needed some concrete plans.

Having a strong belief that the people within the company always know what is wrong and what needs to be fixed, our first act was to schedule a meeting with the top leaders in the company: the directors, vice presidents, and Popeyes leadership team. We went to a nearby conference center to focus on the work that needed to be done.

The people in the room identified the major issues facing the brand.

- Sales, guest transactions, and market share were declining.

- No pipeline of innovative new products existed to draw guests into the restaurant.

- No national media plan existed to tell the guests about our great food.

- We had no compelling advertising message.

- Drive-thru speed of service was dead last in the ranking of quick-service chains.

- Guest ratings were great for our food and weak on virtually all other measures.

- Restaurants were tired and old-looking— in need of a remodel.

- Franchise owners were not making much money—and it was getting worse.

- New restaurants were opening, but were performing poorly.

Other than that, things were going pretty well.

After the team had summarized the top problems that needed to be tackled at Popeyes, I put up a slide of all the current active projects at the company. There were 128. We were busy.

I drew this equation on the flip chart: activity $\neq$ results. Quiet in the room.

When I asked how long the issues facing the brand had existed, a veteran employee named Sondra raised her hand and said, "We put that list up on the wall every year at the offsite meeting."

After I absorbed the implication of her feedback, I asked her, "Would you like to be on the team that actually solves those issues?"

Without missing a beat, she responded, "Oh, yes, I would!"

Of course she would. How can your team be motivated and excited to contribute to the future if they know they are not working on the few vital matters that will lead to superior results?

The Dare-to-Serve Leader must have the courage to focus on and solve the hard things facing the organization. We cannot serve our people well if we lead them through a long list of activities that don't change the performance of the organization. Instead, dare to act on the few game-changing initiatives that will deliver superior performance results.

WHY NOT FIX IT?

Why do leaders resist fixing the hard stuff that stands between mediocre and superior performance?

- Fear of failure?

- Absence of ideas?

- Worries about resources?

- Lack of courage?

I don't know. This I do know. A leader who is unwilling to tackle the real problems and fix them cripples the organization. If the team is not working on the real problems, they often make up work to justify their existence. They sense that their activities will not yield superior results. They become discouraged by the futility of it all. They hide at their desks and await the next round of bad news.

This was the mindset of Popeyes. We were doomed if we stayed on the current course.

DARE-TO-SERVE REFLECTION #7 *What are the few vital things that must be addressed in your organization to drive better performance?*

As the leader, you have followers who are looking for your weaknesses and praying for your strengths. Give them what they pray for—a daring, aspirational plan that fixes real problems and yields results.

COMMIT THE RESOURCES

Unless such commitment is made,
there are only promises and hopes, but no plan.

PETER DRUCKER, *DRUCKER MANAGEMENT*

One of the questions followers have for a leader is, will you put your money where your mouth is? Unfortunately for the people, leaders too often craft bold ambitions without providing resources for the organization to accomplish the vision.

When a leader commits sufficient resources to reach the daring destination, it conveys conviction, determination, and dedication to the goals. This may be the most important test of your leadership from the followers' point of view.

The Popeyes franchisees taught us a lesson on this that we'll never forget.

The leadership team and the ten elected franchise leaders of the Popeyes International Franchising Association—called the PIFA board—met at a Chicago airport hotel. Stuffed in a bad basement conference room, we were planning to ask our franchisees to shift our television advertising from 100 percent locally purchased programming to 100 percent nationally purchased cable programming. It was a bold, unprecedented request. If we accomplished it, our Popeyes message would reach twice as many people.

Our thesis was that national advertising would be the most effective way to accelerate awareness of our Popeyes brand and encourage more people to eat at our restaurants. The challenge for our franchise owners was that we were asking them to let go of their franchisee-controlled media dollars behind local promotions for the benefit of the system as a whole.

The meeting began with an expert—a media guru spoke and provided an analysis of what our television dollars would buy if we shifted local dollars to national television. This gentleman made the case that Popeyes was at a tipping point, and now was the perfect time for shifting to national media.

We expected the franchisees to be highly skeptical of the analysis, but the expert did his job well. He didn't try to put anything over on his audience. He had the facts in hand and spoke in layman's terms. He appeared to have Popeyes' best interests in mind. The franchise owners found him credible.

Next, the Popeyes brand marketing leader presented the idea of three national flights (about nine weeks of advertising in the next twelve months). It was a big dollar commitment—about $12 million. It would require all of the media dollars we had available annually across the entire U.S. system. If it didn't work, we would have used up the entire fund, with nothing in reserve.

We didn't have much proof of concept—Popeyes' prior experiences with national media had been mixed. But the franchisees seemed to understand that we were in a dire situation: our sales trend had been negative for a long time. Popeyes needed to act boldly to get sales moving positively again. We needed to take risks. This is something our entrepreneurs understood all too well.

After our brand marketing leader presented the case, the franchisees asked the Popeyes Leadership Team to leave the room so that they could talk among themselves. We had no way to predict whether we were moving toward war or alliance. We hadn't worked together very long and didn't have a track record of results together. If we reached agreement on this idea, it would be the first bold step we took together.

The time we spent in the hotel hallway seemed like forever. We started talking about what we would do to change the franchise owners' minds if they told us "no." We were working on Plan B.

They finally called us back into the room and said, "If you're so confident in this action, let's go big." Then the surprise: "We don't think nine weeks of advertising is a bold enough plan. We propose thirty-one weeks of national advertising over the next sixteen months. We think we can convince the Popeyes system to commit to this if you (the Popeyes franchisor) agree to invest $6 million in the advertising fund. What do you think?"

It was a test. A test of our conviction behind the idea and our confidence in the bold idea.

The idea they proposed—that the corporate entity, the franchisor, would kick in money to the advertising fund—was unheard of, at Popeyes or anywhere else.

In our business model, franchisees contribute 3 to 4

percent of their total sales to fund Popeyes advertising. The corporation doesn't add to the fund. A $6 million investment in media would have no near-term economic return to Popeyes shareholders and would reduce our earnings by a significant amount in the first year.

How daring were we feeling now?

With some trepidation, the leadership team pitched the idea to the Popeyes board of directors. The presentation was inspired, but the projected results were not a sure bet. We asked the board to take the risk with us and approve this bold investment so that we could demonstrate our conviction to the Popeyes system.

DARE-TO-SERVE REFLECTION #8 *Have you committed the resources needed to reach the daring destination?*

This decision proved to be a true turning point for Popeyes. The corporation made the big investment. The franchisees made the big commitment to move to national advertising. At first, the execution of the plan was imperfect. Thankfully, the following year Popeyes restaurant guest traffic was positive for the first time in seven years. Total sales grew as well.

Five years later, our franchisees would say that this one decision started our brand on a multi-year trajectory of industry-leading performance. They were right. We made a bold decision together—we both took big risks. We put our money where our mouth was, and the strategy won in the marketplace.

BRING OUT THE BEST IN PEOPLE

So much of what we call management consists
in making it difficult for people to work.

PETER DRUCKER

Dare-to-Serve Leaders create work environments that bring out the best in their people. If you have an under-performing team, the easy thing to do is to say, "I need new people." Frankly, that is what most leaders do—fire the people you have and go get new ones.

If you ask the people what constrains their performance, it is usually not skills—it is the work environment established by the leader. The work environment can inspire boldness, innovation, and excellence. Or it can strangle the capability and productivity of the people and the team.

This is the work of the leader: to create a work environment that yields superior results.

After determining the vital few, hard things that needed to be fixed at Popeyes, the leadership team held a second offsite retreat with our leaders. The purpose of this meeting was to build more effective teamwork across the departments of the company.

We played a "game" facilitated by a consultant to teach us how teamwork drives performance. It was a production-line exercise in which groups competed to assemble and decorate an origami paper star called a Starship.

Three teams competed in the exercise. Team 2 was particularly inept at this game, and after three rounds of competition had not produced one single Starship that passed Quality Assurance inspection. At this point, Teams 1 and

3 were laughing at the dysfunction of Team 2. Team 2 asked for a fifteen-minute huddle to reorganize their approach to the game.

When Team 2 returned, their next round of production generated thirty-six Starships and 100 percent of these passed Quality Assurance inspection. This was more than twice the number of Starships produced by either of the other two teams. The room was stunned at the change in Team 2's performance. Curiosity replaced laughter.

We asked Team 2 to explain what had changed the trajectory of their performance. How did they go from laughable to laudable results? They said, "In the first rounds, we just put everyone in a job and basically said, go fast. Then we saw that we had multiple breakdowns. Bottlenecks caused by skill gaps and poor processes. We had people folding paper who couldn't fold paper. We had people coloring Starships who couldn't color. We had people on the sidelines watching but not contributing. We had high achievers cheering but not helping. We were dysfunctional."

"What did you do in the fifteen-minute break?" I asked.

"We asked people what position they thought they were best suited to—and then we placed them in that job. We had the process people re-engineer our process. We had the artistic people color. We had people who folded paper best, fold the paper. We had enthusiastic coaches be enthusiastic coaches. We had timekeepers keep track of time. We encouraged one another and set a bold goal of beating the other two teams. Then we came back to the room and did our best work yet."

The Starship exercise revealed some remarkably simple lessons in leading high-performance teams:

- Find out the strengths of each team member and assign each to a role that uses those strengths.

- Determine the skill gaps on the team and add that capability to the team.

- Respect different talents in the team; everyone has something to contribute.

- Create both the processes and the environment for success.

- The leaders can't create winning results on their own—the team creates the win.

In capturing the lessons of this high-performing Team 2, we decided to make this the new way of working together at Popeyes. We would build a cross-functional team approach to each business strategy on the Roadmap to Results. We would call the teams "Starship Teams."

Here's how the teams were organized: Each team had an executive sponsor, a leadership team member who was available for coaching but not directly involved in leading the team. The teams could seek out any talent they needed from any department in the company—in fact, cross-functional team members were a requirement. Each team chose a process person—called a project management officer (PMO)—to ensure they had a work plan, milestones, and measurable results. Each team leader was coached on how to get the best work from his or her team in a collaborative fashion.

Interestingly, the real-world experiment with Starship Teams had many of the same outcomes of the Starship game at the offsite meeting. We had teams that raced forward with some initial success, but then stalled and had to regroup. We had teams that were completely dysfunctional at the start; then by realizing their thought errors and making corrections, they were able to outperform all the other teams. We had the steady teams that didn't set the world on fire with results at the start, but then, as they grew together as a team, produced better and better outcomes.

Here are the results of the four high-performing Starship Teams.

The *Build a Distinctive Brand* team reinvented the process for new product innovation. They created a research approach that steadily improved the success rate of new items in test markets. They expanded their team to include our most innovative franchise owners with a passion for superior food. In their third year together, the new products conceived by this team led to industry-leading sales results—and Popeyes won a *Nation's Restaurant News* MenuMasters Award for launching the year's most innovative new limited-time offer in quick-service restaurants.

The *Run Great Restaurants* team tackled Popeyes' slow speed of service. They studied the best-in-class competitors and determined that we needed new equipment, new processes, and retraining of our restaurant teams. They created a way to measure progress so we could see results. This team conducted an initial test in one restaurant to see if they had a plan that worked. Then they expanded the test to a few markets to work out the details. When they launched the speed-of-service initiative nationally with new equipment and retrained restaurant teams, we reached our speed goal of 75 percent of restaurants with an average drive-thru speed of 180 seconds or less in one year. Before this initiative, we had been ranked dead last among our competitors on speed. Two years later we were featured in a leading industry publication as the competitor most focused on improved speed of service.

The *Grow Restaurant Profits* team chased cost savings in the supply chain with a goal of saving the system $7 to 10 million—which was about half of a margin point on a restaurant profit and loss (P&L) statement. The team set up a process to examine every segment of the supply chain. They updated product specifications and rebid items to gain better pricing. They surveyed suppliers for savings ideas that would not degrade food quality and compiled a list of ideas with merit. They audited distribution centers and the purchasing processes to make sure cost errors were discovered and fixed. At the end of three years, this team had saved our restaurants more than $40 million, adding two full margin points to an average restaurant P&L.

The *Accelerate Quality Restaurants* team had the most difficult goal—to become an industry leader of new restaurant builds, with high volumes and high returns for the owners who would invest in them. At first it was difficult for this team to be successful, because the other three teams had to improve our current restaurant performance for the franchise owners to be excited about building *new* Popeyes restaurants.

As the saying goes, this team "focused on what they could control." They purchased new site-selection software that immediately helped direct owners to better real estate with strong opening sales performance. This virtually eliminated the "dogs," the high failure rate of our prior new openings.

Using predictive software, the team mapped the top eleven market opportunities so that they could guide owners and resources to the best locations. They redesigned the materials we used to "sell" owners on the new build opportunity—highlighting the exciting returns on investment that the new restaurants were delivering. Last year, Popeyes built more quick-service drive-thru restaurants in the United States than any chain except McDonald's.

DARE-TO-SERVE REFLECTION #9 *What steps have you taken to create a work environment that brings out the best performance from your team?*

Not every team has been as successful as these four. We had three teams that struggled to reach their goals or decided to delay based on new learning. There were no regrets and no failures. This fresh, new way of working produced an exciting, focused workplace where people across the company could contribute their skills to help deliver superior performance. It created an atmosphere that inspired new solutions and improved performance results.

This new way of working also had an unexpected benefit. It produced a cadre of new, high-performing leaders throughout the organization. We now had more opportunities for our leaders to contribute and grow in capability. We included a wider range of leaders in the teams. We gained visibility for our leaders—observing both their competencies and their character traits. Many of the leaders that we "discovered" in this process have been promoted to greater responsibilities.

This better working environment has stimulated people to grow and contribute their best work. It has led to a new level of performance.

THE COURAGE TO MEASURE PROGRESS

You move what you measure.

POPEYES MANTRA

The lack of decision-making information available at Popeyes when I joined the company was startling. Essentially, we tracked dollar sales because that was the basis for collecting royalty payments from our franchise owners. We also had strong accounting processes for public company reporting. Beyond that, we were clueless about the key metrics of our business.

As a result, we had many *passionate* conversations with our franchise owners. Virtually none of those conversations could be corroborated with facts.

We argued about whether our speed of service was as bad as we thought it was. We argued about whether restaurant profits were improving or not. We argued about whether marketing events were successes or failures.

Without data, the truth was not evident. Worse yet, each of us could hide behind our own version of the truth.

Our leadership team decided to go get the data we

needed to inform decision making and measure progress. We didn't know what the data would say. The situation could be better than we thought, or it could be much worse. If we were going to serve the people well, we needed to know exactly where we stood. This required courage, because the facts don't lie.

We continued tracking sales and we added a new measure, market share; our percent of the chicken quick-service restaurant dollar sales. Market share was an important addition, because it told us whether we were gaining or losing position relative to the competition.

We decided to install equipment to measure speed of service at our drive-thru windows, and we began collecting the average speed of service every week, for every restaurant.

We designed and fielded our first-ever guest-experience monitor—a survey that our guests used to tell us how we were doing. Within six months, we had guest feedback from every restaurant in the system.

Our biggest data gap was measuring restaurant operating profits. We had profitability data on only a few dozen company-owned restaurants, but none from our franchise-owned restaurants. When we began collecting individual restaurant P&L statements, it was delivered in disparate ways—from computer downloads, Excel spreadsheets, or even handwritten charts. We hired a newly minted college graduate to trudge through the files, clean up the data, and make summary tables that we could analyze. After two years, we finally had a meaningful set of data to track profitability progress and analyze our business decisions. This was the single biggest hurdle we overcame. We could now evaluate our performance by the same measure the franchise owner used—restaurant operating profits.

We then started collecting data on the performance of our new restaurants, tracking return on investment. The predictive software tool we had purchased reduced the failure rate of new restaurants by helping owners find better real estate sites. The financial tracking data proved that those new restaurants were now achieving better return.

DARE-TO-SERVE REFLECTION #10 *What are the milestones and measurements of progress in your organization? Are you acting on what you learn from the data?*

The most courageous aspect of collecting this new data was our decision to report the data publicly to our employees, our franchise owners, our board, and our shareholders. We made a commitment that we would share the results, good or bad.

What was so important about establishing these new measures of performance?

- The numbers don't lie. Once you actually know the truth, you can start improving.

- The numbers don't lie. The numbers hold you accountable to making real improvements.

- The numbers don't lie. The numbers inspire you to make action plans for reaching goals.

Take note: measurements matter only if you plan to *act* upon what you learn. At Popeyes, we established routines to look at the data regularly and to adjust our plans if we fell short of the goals.

This sounds really basic. However, measuring progress, reporting results, and adjusting to the feedback was essential to improving Popeyes performance. Measures held the team accountable for progress. Leadership is being courageous enough to measure and report performance results—to be accountable. This attention to accountability improves the odds of superior results.

PLAUSIBILITY OF THE GOALS

One potential thought error to watch out for with the daring destination is *plausibility*. The destination and goals that you set for the team, while challenging them to stretch and grow, must be achievable.

At Popeyes, one of the ways we determined the future state of the enterprise was to study our best competitors carefully. What sales and profit levels did they achieve? What guest satisfaction scores represented best-in-class? What level of restaurant operating profit was above average, yet reachable?

This process of testing our daring aspirations to be sure they could be achieved was a critical step. If the destination had been hopelessly unrealistic, the team would not have believed in it. They would have held back their best work until there was evidence that this turnaround was real. Instead, they heard the business case behind the bold plan and they determined that success was *possible*.

Your team needs a clear understanding of how you define the daring destination—a business case that is compelling and gives them confidence to proceed.

WHAT IS THE DARING DESTINATION?—SUPERIOR RESULTS

When we started with the daring destination for Popeyes, we had no idea if we would be successful. Looking back, the performance results have been stunning. We have led the organization to five years of growth in market share and sales. We have faster service at our drive-thrus. Restaurant profits and new restaurant returns are now in the top tier of our industry.

No other quick-service restaurant has delivered comparable results during this time frame. Our primary chicken competitor has experienced significant declines in sales, restaurant profits, and total number of restaurants in the United States.

In 2013, we reached the daring destination we had defined back in 2007. Popeyes franchise owners have been well served by these business results. The improved

Popeyes Performance Results

Average restaurant performance

	2008	2013	Results
Restaurant sales ($ millions)	1.0	1.25	Exceeded goal
Share of chicken quick-service (%)	14	21	Exceeded goal
Speed of service at drive-thru (seconds)	225+	180	Achieved
Restaurant operating profit (%)	18	22	Achieved
New restaurant owner returns (%)	< 10	≈ 25	Achieved

performance of the restaurants has built their confidence in Popeyes' future. As such, the franchise owners have chosen to invest in that future by remodeling the existing restaurants and building new restaurants at a rapid pace.

DARING AND SERVING GO TOGETHER

Dare-to-Serve Leaders challenge their followers with bold, courageous, exciting aspirations. The daring destination is designed to benefit the people and the enterprise, not just the leader.

The destination is a compelling, strategic roadmap with specific goals and action plans. It is focused on the vital few things that will drive superior performance. It has measurements and milestones to track progress that are reported to the public.

The Dare-to-Serve Leader creates an environment where the people grow while pursuing the daring aspiration, gaining new confidence and valuable skills. On the way to the destination, the people are drawn together as an effective team. This leads to the desired outcome of a team performing at the highest level, driving results that cannot be produced by the leader alone.

With the courage of the dare—and the humility of the leader—daring destinations serve the people well.

THREE

WHY DO WE DO THIS WORK?

Most of us . . . have jobs that are too small for our spirits.
STUDS TERKEL, *WORKING*

WHY DOES WORK have such a bad reputation? Or is it just my line of work that has a bad reputation?

When you work in the restaurant business, you take a lot of flak for your job—particularly if you work in "fast food." Popular culture is full of unflattering references, such as "burger flipper" and "minimum-wage worker." Despite the fact that one in ten Americans currently works in a restaurant, one-third of Americans find their first job in a restaurant, and 50 percent of Americans work in a restaurant at some point in their working lives, restaurant work is regarded with disdain.

This drives me crazy. I know amazing people who work in the restaurant business. They deserve respect and dignity for what they do for a living. They feed people. They develop leaders. They help kids get through high school. They give people first and second chances for employment. They serve people kindly. They teach and counsel team members. They create jobs. They give generously in the community. They give the best of themselves to the people and the communities they serve.

Could we acknowledge and appreciate the purposeful, meaningful, valuable, and important work that restaurant people do?

Once I was visiting a top-performing restaurant manager in Chicago. She was full of positive energy for her work, and I asked her, "What is it that you love about this job?" She smiled and said, "Cheryl, I have the best job ever. I am a teacher, a counselor, a social worker, a mom, a minister, a finance advisor, and more. You see, in this position, I have the opportunity to impact the lives of young people just starting out. I help them get their grades up so that they can go to college. I teach them job skills so they can pay their bills. I help them solve problems when they don't have friends or family to help. I can't imagine a more important job in this community." For this restaurant manager, work has meaning and purpose.

Consider this thought: *It is the leader's responsibility to bring purpose and meaning to the work of the organization.*

Purpose and meaning are essential to creating a high-performance organization. When people believe their work matters, they contribute differently. They arrive early and stay late. They find creative solutions to problems. They build their skills so they can add more value. They work collaboratively to ensure the success of the team. They stay in the job longer.

Purpose and meaning at work raise the energy level, commitment, and performance of the team.

WHY DOES MEANING MATTER?

The Gallup organization publishes a study each year called *State of the American Workplace: Employee Engagement Insights for U.S. Business Leaders.* The 2013 study states that 30 percent of the U.S. workforce are engaged in their work. Of course, this means 70 percent of the workforce are not engaged in their work. More than twice as many people are "checked-out" as are "checked-in."

Gallup's study goes on to explain that the companies with the top 25 percent of engagement scores (top quartile) have significantly higher productivity, profitability, customer ratings, and less employee turnover. Gallup estimates that actively disengaged employees cost the U.S. economy $450 to 550 billion per year.

I've been reading this study every year it has been published since the year 2000. The statistics haven't changed much. The only thing I can conclude is that *leaders* haven't changed much.

What are two of Gallup's recommendations to increase employee engagement?

- Hire the right leaders, who support and engage their teams.

- Encourage leaders to connect with each employee; each person has different needs.

Gallup concludes by saying, "Know that every interaction with an employee has the potential to influence engagement and inspire discretionary effort."

What can a leader do to drive engagement? Help

people find purpose and meaning at work. Until you do, the people are just biding their time, paying their bills, and waiting for something better to come along.

THE WORK THAT WE DO

As part of the turnaround of Popeyes, we decided that the organization should have clarity about the purpose of the work we do. Our leadership team came together, looked at our experiences in this industry, reviewed the values and beliefs we have about restaurant careers, and thought about the role we have in developing leaders.

The conversation started with these beliefs:

> We are proud of the career paths our industry offers. Many of our franchise owners began as a fry cook or front counter person and are now successful entrepreneurs owning multiple restaurants. Many of our restaurant general managers started at the front counter and now run a restaurant business with sales of more than $1.2 million annually. We develop leaders in this business—and we celebrate that fact.
>
> We are proud of the quality of food that our teams prepare each day for our guests. We are proud of the training that we offer to teach people good work habits, food sanitation skills, teamwork, and problem solving. We are proud that we earn our living serving other people—our owners, our team members, our guests. We are proud of the opportunities we bring to developing countries around the globe. We are in the service industry—and we celebrate that fact.

This discussion led us to declare the *purpose* of our work at Popeyes: *Inspire servant leaders to achieve superior results.* We decided that servant leadership would be our philosophy. This makes sense. We are in the business of serving others a delicious meal. Why not lead from the same vantage point?

Servant leadership simply means *service above self*. We decided to serve others well.

Superior results are the measure of how well we serve. Serving and performing go hand in hand.

We created the Popeyes purpose in the fall of 2011, nearly three years after we had begun the turnaround of the company. Why did we choose that time?

The turnaround was well under way. We had begun to experience some success in the bold, ambitious goals we had set for the enterprise. We were serving our franchise owners well, but we were not sure that the success would continue. We worried that we would be just another "one-hit wonder" leadership team who came together for a few years and generated good results and then went our separate ways. What could we do to lead the organization to sustainable success?

While we believed that the work we were doing was purposeful, we weren't sure the rest of the organization shared our conviction. Maybe it was purposeful for us but "just a job" for them.

We analyzed what we had done well and what we needed to do next. We realized that we had not explained to our followers why the work we were doing was important—why we passionately believed in the future of Popeyes. The organization as a whole needed to share in that purpose. At the very next company meeting, we revealed our newly crafted Popeyes purpose to the team:

Popeyes Purpose: *Inspire servant leaders to achieve superior results.*

THE PLAQUE PROBLEM

The Popeyes purpose was well received by the people. We had to spend a fair amount of time explaining servant leadership—helping them understand that it simply meant service to others above self. Other than that, people seemed to understand the purpose. They thought it was laudable. I'm not sure what they said privately after the meeting. I suspect it was something like, "Let's see if this purpose really changes the way we work at Popeyes."

We ran into what every company runs into. Purpose statements are nice. A few people get excited about them and live them in their daily work. Most people leave them right where they saw them—on the plaque on the wall.

Plaques hang on walls. Plaques collect dust. Plaques don't drive superior performance results.

Popeyes people weren't against the purpose, they just had no personal connection to the statement.

I began to challenge the leaders of the company in one-on-one meetings and in large groups. I said, "That purpose statement is a plaque at Popeyes. It hangs on the wall. Alone, it has no meaning and no impact on our performance. The only Popeyes purpose anyone ever meets is YOUR purpose."

No one ever met a plaque. No one ever gave a plaque credit for inspiring them to serve, for helping them reach their potential, or for driving superior results. Plaques don't do that. *People do.*

JOURNEY TO PERSONAL PURPOSE

[Work] is about a search . . . for daily meaning
as well as daily bread.

STUDS TERKEL, *WORKING*

At Popeyes we've been conducting an experiment. It is in the early stages, but the results look promising. We have asked each Popeyes team member to develop a personal purpose. The process begins with a workshop we call Journey to Personal Purpose.

During a one-day session, a facilitator takes the participants through a series of exercises to help discover their core motivation—a *purpose* that gives their work meaning beyond the paycheck. The class starts with an overview of our Popeyes purpose: sharing perspective on what servant leadership is and why we believe it is the most powerful path to superior performance results.

Then the class gets personal.

Journey to Personal Purpose Exercise 1: Lifeline

The leader asks team members to draw a timeline of the significant events of their life that have shaped who they are as a leader, identifying three to five seminal moments, events, or experiences that have shaped their approach to work and leadership.

Perhaps they were a middle child or "the baby" in the family—and this birth order has contributed to who they are and how they approach leadership.

Perhaps there was a traumatic event in their life— the loss of a parent, an illness, an accident—that sent them in a new direction, good or bad, and profoundly shaped their view of the world and of work.

Perhaps there were certain people who mentored them—a teacher, an uncle, a manager at their first job—people who taught them important things that they want to evidence in their work and leadership.

Perhaps they had a difficult job or boss at an early age and that has shaped who they want to be as a leader.

Each participant fills in their "lifeline" chart with three to five key events and then they share their lifeline with a small group. At most workshops, this conversation is full of genuine emotion as the participants share those life experiences that fundamentally define who they are.

DARE-TO-SERVE REFLECTION #11 *How well do you know the people who work for you? Do you know the three or four events of their lives that have shaped who they are today?*

Journey to Personal Purpose Exercise 2: Values Clarification

The second activity is a "card game" to help prioritize the most important values and beliefs that people bring to the workplace and to leadership. For this exercise, we use a deck of cards from the John Maxwell Company that list thirty-four values with a one-sentence definition of each. The deck includes blank cards, allowing participants to add a value if they don't find one of their most important values in the stack.

Individuals start by picking their top-ten priority values. Then they study that stack of ten cards and choose the three values that are most important at work. This process is a real struggle for people. They always ask, "Do I have to narrow the list to three values?"

The class facilitator tells them that if either "family" or "faith/religion" is a top value, they may set those off to the side—know they are high importance—but focus their efforts on selecting the next three values that they want to evidence at work.

This step seems to magically focus people on their top three values for work and leadership.

Why is this exercise so important? We all have values, beliefs, and convictions. Yet few people can articulate their top-priority values when asked. Too often, we speak in generalities, saying words that we think others want to hear. We want to be thought of as honest, genuine, trustworthy, and about thirty other things. But when we are honest with ourselves, we aren't really focused on any particular value at work. We are simply attempting to be good people, doing the best that we can.

As a leader, knowing the values of your team members helps you understand their convictions and their motivations. This understanding can lead to more open conversations and less conflict and misunderstanding.

DARE-TO-SERVE REFLECTION #12 *If you knew the top-priority values of the people on your team, how would you lead more effectively?*

Journey to Personal Purpose Exercise 3: StandOut Roles

The third activity in a Journey to Personal Purpose workshop is a process to discover, uncover, and celebrate the talents of each person. For this exercise we use an online assessment tool called StandOut, created by author and researcher Marcus Buckingham. The assessment determines the primary and secondary roles where the participants' talents and skills are maximized. The report makes them aware of the ways they can best contribute at work and gives them tips on how to use these strengths to their advantage.

DARE-TO-SERVE REFLECTION #13 *Most leaders can tell you the weaknesses of their team members. But can you cite the strengths and talents of your team? Are you accessing their very best capability?*

At Popeyes, we believe every individual is uniquely designed with strengths that they bring to the workplace. If people do not know their own talents and their leader doesn't know them either, we cannot put people in a position for success. As I often remark, "I must know you to grow you."

StandOut Roles are the person's *superpowers*, the best traits to contribute to the team. We ask each person to think about how their talents support their personal purpose. We want them to bring their best capabilities to the table to help drive superior performance.

Journey to Personal Purpose Exercise 4: Personal Purpose

After completing these three exercises—life experiences, values, and strengths—we take team members through a process to craft their personal purpose for work. This is the statement, in one or two sentences, that describes why they come to work each day and how they will positively impact the organization.

The personal purpose statement answers these inquiries:

Throughout my life and work experience, I've discovered these key themes . . .

My top three values are . . .

My StandOut strengths are . . .

My personal purpose for leadership is . . .

My purpose can serve the organization by . . .

Very few people get their purpose done by the end of the workshop. Most will want to let it simmer for a few days, weeks, or months, checking to make sure it has real meaning—they want a purpose that will make a difference in work and leadership. This takes time, as it should. It is too important to rush.

DARE-TO-SERVE REFLECTION #14 *What would happen if you helped your team discover and pursue their personal purpose? How would they contribute differently to the performance of the team?*

Personal **Purpose**

Throughout my life/work experience
I've discovered these key themes:

- _____
- _____
- _____

My top three values:

- _____
- _____
- _____

My StandOut strengths:

- _____
- _____
- _____

My personal purpose for leadership is:

_____

_____

_____

_____

My purpose can serve the organization by:

_____

_____

_____

_____

Your role as a leader is to encourage team members to complete their statements, sharing your own perspective on how meaningful purpose has been to you. Let them know you are looking forward to talking about their personal purpose. This tells them you are interested in them and value their contributions.

The Journey to Personal Purpose exercise and instructions can be found at www.daretoserveleaders.com.

THE IMPACT OF PERSONAL PURPOSE

When a team member lands on their personal purpose, it helps them determine how they connect with the Popeyes Purpose: how will they inspire servant leaders to achieve superior results? What follows are several personal purpose statements from Popeyes leaders. They are diverse and distinctly personal. In every case, their personal purpose has had a positive impact on the performance of Popeyes.

"My purpose is to unleash each individual's unique gift to drive innovation." Dick leads a team of creative people. Creative people can be a challenge to lead—each person a different personality, each of them a bit tender to criticism. Dick's job is to bring out of this team inspired, innovative ideas for Popeyes, such as new menu items, new packaging, new seating designs, and new advertising. This talented team identifies, explores, and executes bold new ideas to grow sales for Popeyes. Dick's personal purpose has "unleashed" industry-leading innovation for Popeyes because of his passion for creating an environment where creative people thrive.

"My purpose is to inspire others to build positive, healthy

relationships to better serve the community." Alice has responsibility for overseeing our supply chain and quality-assurance functions. In this role, she leads teams to seek fresh, innovative solutions for a host of Popeyes challenges. Alice loves to solve problems in teams. She has created an award called the "Can-Do" award to celebrate people who build positive relationships that help solve Popeyes problems. Her purpose has helped us access $40 million in savings for our system, which has significantly improved profit margins at our restaurants.

"My purpose is to create safe work environments where people can take risks and grow to their full potential." Andrew's lifeline reminded him that he has worked in some toxic environments over the years—places that discouraged him and inhibited the performance of the team. Andrew has decided to be a different kind of leader, a leader who provides a healthy environment for taking risks and learning new things. The atmosphere in his department is a lovely combination of high expectations and encouraging words. The people are stretching and taking risks and they are growing in capability. Since Andrew arrived at Popeyes, the performance results of his team have accelerated. I don't think this is a coincidence.

"My purpose is to inspire others to know that it's never too late to live, to love, to matter." ZR's early life was not easy. He witnessed injustice and discrimination in the life of his grandfather. He experienced tragedy when his mother was killed. He struggled with navigating life and work. But instead of declaring defeat, ZR has declared victory. Today he serves as vice president of operations at Popeyes. He has determined that his top three values are Sac-

rifice (it's not about me), Timing (it's never too late), and Redemption (grace and forgiveness). These values have led him to the conclusion that every person deserves to be left whole, no matter what their circumstances. ZR's personal purpose today is to inspire those with difficult starts in life—to understand that it is never too late *to live, to love, to matter.* The impact? He is a beloved coach in our restaurants.

"My purpose is to inspire others to passionately share and pursue their big ideas." Kelsey grew up as a middle child in a family of six children in a small town called Highlands, North Carolina. Kelsey's ideas and ambitions were bigger than her town, and when she graduated from high school, she moved to the city and began pursuing those dreams. Looking back, Kelsey remembers that it was hard to find her voice and confidence from that middle-child position. At work today, as Popeyes internal communications leader, she encourages and supports people with big ideas. Through her work, she gives voice to the big ideas we are making happen at Popeyes.

Each person who discovers and applies their unique personal purpose brings the best of themselves to work. Through the personal purpose process, the person better understands how they connect to the purpose of Popeyes. That leads them to contribute more intentionally to the performance of Popeyes.

SHARING PERSONAL PURPOSE

After a team member develops a personal purpose, the first thing the supervisor encourages them to do is to share it with others. This has proven to be critical. When they share their personal purpose with others, these benefits occur:

1. They receive positive feedback, encouragement, and suggestions from people who have worked side by side with them. This helps confirm and polish the purpose so that it is genuine and actionable.

2. Their coworkers gain a deeper understanding of who they are and how they best contribute at work. As a result, the coworkers know when to ask for their help and contribution to the team.

3. They gain support from their coworkers. A personal purpose helps the team know their strengths and motivations. In turn, the team becomes their *advocate* more often than their critic.

4. They feel a part of something greater than themselves and accountable to contribute their best.

ACTING ON PERSONAL PURPOSE

A personal purpose is just a piece of paper until it is put into action in daily life. At Popeyes, the leaders who have an action plan for their personal purpose are having more impact on the business. We've found that the best practice is to have team members bring their personal purpose action plan to their annual and mid-year performance reviews. These are good times to review their purpose, encourage them to put it into action, and discuss specific ways to act on the purpose in the upcoming months.

Dare-to-Serve Leaders help their followers discover their personal purpose. This builds intentionality, engagement, and leads to positive outcomes, including superior results.

Don't believe me. Ask around. Find a few people who have a well-defined personal purpose. Then look at their contribution to the team and the enterprise. Look at their results. It is no accident.

Personal purpose leads to sustained superior performance. When you know why you come to work, you show up differently. You are more intentional in what you do. You care more about the outcomes. You give your best efforts. This is what the term "highly engaged" looks like at work.

DISCOVERING WHY WE WORK BRINGS SUPERIOR RESULTS

We measure employee engagement to discover the personal connection of our people to Popeyes. There are many drivers of team member engagement; personal purpose is only one of them. As such, we do not have a perfect measure. Nonetheless, I would argue that the Popeyes Employee Engagement Index is the best indicator we have to measure the impact of personal purpose on performance.

Using an independent research firm that is expert in measuring employee engagement, Popeyes conducts an annual study. The Popeyes Employee Engagement Index is a statistical compilation of these four statements:

I am proud to work for Popeyes.

I rarely think about looking for a new job with another company.

I would recommend Popeyes as a great place to work.

Overall, I am extremely satisfied with Popeyes as a place to work.

The firm that measures the Popeyes Employee Engagement Index reports that our overall score of 78 percent is significantly above the norm of 69 percent for their other client companies. The top 25 percent of our leaders, those with the highest engagement index scores, excel at 89 percent. These above-average scores for employee engagement are evidence of the personal purpose culture we are building at Popeyes.

Popeyes Engagement Results

	Total Popeyes (%)	Top 25% of Popeyes Leaders (%)
2012 Popeyes Employee Engagement Index	78	89

HELP THOSE WHO WANT TO BE HELPED

At Popeyes, we have found that personal purpose makes a difference for the organization. Personal purpose clarifies where the people stand and unleashes their talent.

Even so, we can only help those who want to be helped. Personal purpose is only effective for those who *want* to have purpose and meaning in their life. It is not for everybody. Many people go through life without a personal purpose—and they don't mind at all.

We have had several leaders opt out of the journey to

personal purpose. And we let them. This problem takes care of itself over time. Those who have no clear personal purpose are not highly engaged and typically do not contribute their best work. Eventually they leave or are asked to leave the organization. And the organization becomes stronger.

Helping people who want to find meaning and purpose at work is exceptionally rewarding. It is the leader's opportunity to leave a legacy in the lives of the people you lead.

Personal purpose accelerates employee engagement and the performance of the organization.

FOUR

HOW WILL WE **WORK TOGETHER**?

Alone we can do so little; together we can do so much.

HELEN KELLER

THE TURNAROUND OF A TEAM'S performance or a company's performance requires a compelling strategic plan—a roadmap that gives clarity about *what* the team or company will do to get to the daring destination we talked about in chapter 2. This well-defined business plan is essential to help an organization grow. Without it, the team will fail.

A strategic roadmap is *essential*, but it is *insufficient* to drive superior results.

As important as *what* you decide to do, is to decide *how* you will work together to accomplish the plan. What principles will guide the daily work of the team, enabling them to serve one another and the business plan well? What principles, when put into action, will lead to superior results?

Some call this the *culture* of the organization—which is a good word for it, because it means the way we think, behave, and work together to accomplish goals. Defining the principles of the culture and holding the team accountable to those principles is fundamentally the work and the responsibility of the leader.

Done well, principles are the fuel for accelerating the team's performance. Without principles in action, the leader cannot drive superior results—and may, in fact, risk disaster.

DARE-TO-SERVE REFLECTION #15 *What are the principles of your organization? Are they evident in the daily actions of the team members?*

The many ethical debacles in major corporations in the last two decades have increased my zeal for principled leadership. Enron Corporation claimed the four values of Respect, Integrity, Communication, and Excellence in their corporate documents and plaques. In a *New York Times* article, James Kunen quotes a person who commented on the reality of Enron's corporate values, saying, "Why not just come right out and say it? 'We will strive to make as much money as we can without going to prison.'"

For principles to matter, they have to be "in action," not on plaques. Principles must come alive in the daily conversations, decisions, and actions of the team.

POPEYES PRINCIPLES

At Popeyes, we chose six principles to help us work together. These principles guide our daily actions and support our purpose: *to inspire servant leaders to achieve superior results.*

We are passionate about what we do.

We listen carefully and learn continuously.

We are fact-based and planful.

We coach and develop our people.

We are personally accountable.

We value humility.

Far more important than the words on the plaque, however, is the *use* of these principles in our daily work. Let's look at examples of how we work together at Popeyes, using these six principles.

We are passionate about what we do

Nothing great was ever achieved without enthusiasm.

RALPH WALDO EMERSON, *ESSAYS: FIRST SERIES*

At Popeyes, our first principle is—*we are passionate about what we do.* We don't define the specifics of what passion looks like for you. We just want you to have it. As leaders, our passion is the fuel that inspires people to move toward a bold ambition for the organization.

We decided that this principle of passion was particularly important to a franchise organization. Popeyes franchisees have a lot of passion—and they should. They made a huge decision to invest in the Popeyes business— they are "all in." As a result, they care deeply about the decisions that impact their business. That passion deserves respect.

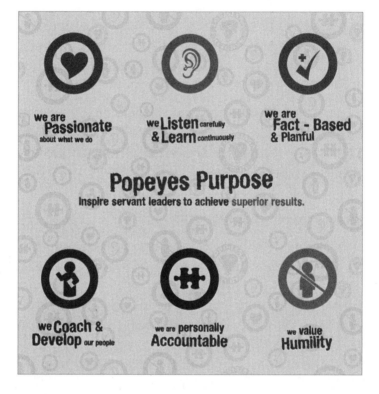

A few years ago, we presented a new design for remodeling Popeyes restaurants. We took ten franchise owners to see the prototypes of the new building and dining room in New Orleans. We were excited to reveal the future look of the brand.

The franchise owners hated the new look. In their view, it was not contemporary enough. It cost too much. It didn't stand up well to the new designs of Starbucks and McDonald's. They were passionate. They had a strong point of view: they did not support this remodel.

The Popeyes Leadership Team was terribly disappointed in their response, and we were inclined to argue our point of view. Instead, we respected the passion of the franchise owners. We wanted the franchise leaders to be enthusiastic and committed to the new restaurant design, for they would inspire the whole Popeyes system to remodel. Lack of passion for the new design would doom the results of the remodel program.

DARE-TO-SERVE REFLECTION #16 *How is passion demonstrated in the daily actions of you and your team?*

We accepted the franchise owners' feedback. We started over on the design and two years later presented a contemporary, strong remodel design that the franchisees loved at first sight. The franchise owners' passion for this new look led our system to remodel 80 percent of our restaurants in a two-year period, a task that would typically have taken five or more years. Passion drove performance results.

Dare-to-Serve Leaders welcome passion to the team. Passion is the fuel of the organization—it drives superior performance.

We listen carefully and learn continuously

Don't assume, because you are intelligent,
able, and well-motivated, that you are open
to communication, that you know how to listen.

ROBERT K. GREENLEAF, *SERVANT LEADERSHIP*

When my daughter Tracy was thirteen, she began behaving as most teenagers do. She broke the rules. She talked back. She slept late. She came home late. She left wet towels on the floor.

But her most annoying teenager behavior?

When I attempted to tell her something, she would put a finger in each ear to block the sound of my voice and say, "Mini-headphones . . . can't hear you . . ."

Somewhere along the way to adulthood, we tend to stop listening and learning from others. In fact, it's worse than that. As adults, we start telling everybody what to do—and we call it leadership.

Wrong answer.

What gets in the way of listening and learning? It's simple. As leaders, we want to think that we have all the answers. Having all the answers makes us feel indispensable to the organization and secure in our jobs.

Unfortunately, nothing could be further from the truth.

Andy Stanley, pastor of our Atlanta church, says it this way: "The leader's IQ declines with every promotion."

With every promotion, the leader gets further from the people, further from the facts, and further from the insights he or she needs to lead. Listening carefully and learning continuously are the antidote for our distance from reality.

At Popeyes we chose *We listen carefully and learn continuously* as our second principle because we knew we would need frequent reminders to listen to our franchisees and we knew we would need to learn from our mistakes.

For example, a few months ago we had a difficult matter come up about sourcing a particular product for our restaurants—a supply chain problem. There was a significant difference of opinion between the leaders of Popeyes and the franchise leaders who oversee the Popeyes purchasing and distribution cooperative.

The Popeyes Leadership Team was mad about the matter.

When leaders get mad, listening and learning go out the window. Mad leaders know exactly what they want to say. They cut to the chase and tell you exactly how they feel—which is highly efficient but very ineffective. The unfortunate truth: efficiency with people ruins relationships.

Our leadership team caught ourselves going down the wrong path and reconsidered our principle. We envisioned the outcome of a "mad meeting" where everyone leaves with steam coming out of their ears and nothing is solved. We needed to choose a better path. We decided we would be less direct with our concerns at the beginning of the meeting. We would ask questions to clarify, and spend time listening carefully to the franchise owners' point of view.

Our brains said to this idea, "How slow and inefficient." Yet our principle prevailed—*listen and learn*.

DARE-TO-SERVE REFLECTION #17 *Are you and your team listening carefully and learning continuously from the people you serve?*

We opened the meeting with a friendly exchange. We asked open-ended questions to gather more information about the issue. We learned some things we did not know that changed our understanding of the matter. We found the franchise owners more open to new ideas than we expected. They were willing to consider some new approaches to find a better solution together.

Over the course of a few days of follow-up conversations, the problem was resolved in a way that was acceptable to all parties. Listening and learning provided the path to a superior outcome for all.

It's not a natural instinct, but a Dare-to-Serve Leader pauses—listens carefully and learns continuously—before taking action. Invariably, this helps the people reach alignment on the next steps so that they can execute them with excellence. This leads to a better outcome than a leader's unilateral decision.

We are fact-based and planful

There are abundant current examples of loss of leadership that stems from a failure to foresee what reasonably could have been foreseen, and from failure to act on that knowledge while the leader had freedom to act.

ROBERT K. GREENLEAF, *SERVANT LEADERSHIP*

You may be surprised to see a principle about being "fact-based and planful." It sounds more like a process for doing business than a principle. At Popeyes we chose to make this a principle because it has revolutionized the way we work. Better facts and better planning have built trust and alignment with our franchise owners. Perhaps we could have called this principle "collaborate," for that is the true benefit of being fact-based and planful—it enables collaboration.

As I mentioned earlier, at the beginning of the turnaround, we had no financial data on the performance of our restaurants. As a result, we didn't know if the marketing promotions we used to drive sales were profitable to the owners or not. We needed facts.

A year later, a veteran franchisee chastised our leadership team by saying that the June promotion had nearly bankrupted the Popeyes system because we discounted our core menu meals. I paused for a moment and then said calmly, "Actually, the Popeyes system had its highest absolute dollar profits in June of any promotion in the past year." The franchise owner asked me how I knew that to be true. I said, "Because we have over 1,000 restaurant P&Ls in hand." He smiled and said, "Then you actually know!"

Facts remove whim and personal opinion from the decision process. Over time, facts build trust, alignment, and effective collaboration with the people we serve. Planning has a similar effect.

DARE-TO-SERVE REFLECTION #18 *What process do you have for collecting and analyzing the facts? What process do you have for planning the future?*

We used to plan Popeyes marketing promotions from month to month and we were in a constant cycle of meetings to pick the next promotion. It was exhausting, and our picks didn't perform very well. Today we have a three-year planning process for promotions. We have built a promotion calendar that is organized by what sells in each season. We have agreed on how many new products we need each year and they are tested and proven before launch. The calendar-planning meeting is highly organized, the promotions are chosen based on factual data, and our success rate has improved dramatically.

Planning reduces last-minute decisions. Rushed decisions are often the wrong decisions.

The Dare-to-Serve Leader gathers the facts needed for decision making and builds a planning process. In doing so, the leader builds trust, alignment, and collaboration with the people served. Over time, the better-considered decisions and more thoughtful plans lead to improved performance results.

We coach and develop our people

*To put it simply and starkly: If you don't get
the people process right, you will never fulfill
the potential of your business.*

LARRY BOSSIDY, RETIRED CEO OF ALLIED SIGNAL

When we chose this fourth principle at Popeyes—*We
coach and develop our people*—it was for a different reason
than all the others. Our study of servant leadership had
convinced us that coaching and developing people was a
signature trait of a servant leader company, but it was not
a core competency at Popeyes. Developing our people
was, in general, an afterthought.

We had good excuses. The restaurant business is 24/7.

DARE-TO-SERVE REFLECTION #19 *What is your
coaching routine? Do you have a specific
and thoughtful development plan for
each of your team members?*

The leadership team works long hours: we travel from
city to city visiting our restaurants and solving problems.
When would we find time for coaching and developing
people, other than in a once-a-year performance review?

In feedback sessions, our people told us we that we had
significant opportunities for growing, developing, and
recognizing our people.

Our first step was to hire human resource professionals
to develop basic people practices. We then began to put
resources behind our aspirational principle.

We now do a good job of setting performance objectives and preparing annual development plans for each person. We review our talent on a regular basis and look for assignments to challenge our top performers. We encourage supervisors to have biweekly one-on-one coaching sessions with those who report to them to clarify expectations, ask coaching questions, and process decisions in a timely manner. We offer leadership development workshops to increase capabilities.

We believe this is just the beginning of becoming a company that has top-tier coaching and development. Our next step will be to teach a common coaching model to all of our leaders in order to advance this competency in the organization.

We aren't where we want to be on the coaching and development principle. I share this with you to be completely transparent with the Popeyes story. We do some principles very well but we still have a long way to go in other areas. I believe if you have a principle that you know is critical to driving superior performance, you have to say so—even if you fall short on that principle today.

We are going to become a company that is known for its leadership development because we have conviction about the principle of coaching and developing leaders. This principle will hold us accountable to drive change in our daily actions over time.

We are personally accountable

The price of greatness is responsibility.

WINSTON CHURCHILL,

SPEECH AT HARVARD UNIVERSITY, 1943

Each Popeyes principle has a visual symbol—the symbol for personal accountability is a puzzle piece. We chose this symbol to communicate the importance of each person doing "their piece of the puzzle." That is what personal accountability looks like—a puzzle where all the pieces lock together to form a picture.

We want our Popeyes leaders and our franchise owners to do what they say they are going to do—to live up to their promises. We want them to own the roles and responsibilities of their job. We want them to quickly fess up and ask forgiveness if they make a mistake. We want them to solve the problems they discover, not deny responsibility or point fingers and blame.

This principle is inherently important in a franchisor-franchisee partnership. The business model would not work if either one of us were to shirk our accountabilities.

For example . . . When a franchisor lacks accountability for building the brand or the operating system, the franchisees' business suffers and they cannot overcome the problem on their own. When the franchisees fail to treat guests well or serve quality food, the franchisor and the brand are damaged and cannot overcome the issue without action on the franchise owner's part. Our business is designed as a symbiotic relationship—a partnership. Accountability is required.

Other businesses may be structured differently, but

every business requires collaboration among people to execute the business plan. I can't think of a business where one leader, acting alone, can deliver superior performance. We all operate in interdependent teams that rely on each team member or each department to do their piece of the puzzle.

DARE-TO-SERVE REFLECTION #20 *How do you hold your team accountable and discourage victim mindsets or blaming others? How does your team hold you personally accountable?*

The Dare-to-Serve Leader understands the critical importance of personal accountability in reaching superior performance.

We value humility

Ego can't sleep. It micro-manages. It disempowers.
It reduces our capability. It excels in control.
STEPHEN COVEY

At Popeyes, you will often hear this phrase: "If you say you are humble, you are not."

Humility is the toughest principle to talk about and the toughest principle to do. If you *talk* about humility, you might look as though you *think* you are humble. Your team will be quick to notice the examples of when you are not humble. If you aspire to *be* humble in your daily actions, you will struggle to be consistent. Your team will be quick to notice this as well.

When the Popeyes Leadership Team was developing our six principles for serving others, this principle was nonnegotiable for all of us. It belonged on our plaque. We wanted humility to be evident in our daily actions.

Why? Our career experiences had yielded this common conclusion: leaders without humility are hell to work for. They are concerned primarily with themselves. They rarely consider the views or needs of others.

DARE-TO-SERVE REFLECTION #21 *How do you and your team model humility in your daily actions?*

We agreed that we are not naturally humble either. That means there are plenty of days we are hell to work for, too. Therefore, humility *must* be a principle that we have conviction about—or we will never demonstrate humility to our teams. This principle will forever be an aspiration, not an accomplishment. As hard as we try, we will repeatedly fall short.

Humble leaders inspire, but self-centered leaders squash the spirit of the people. Dare-to-Serve Leaders *aspire* to be more humble.

HOW WE WORK TOGETHER FOR SUPERIOR RESULTS

Does Dare-to-Serve Leadership work? Does it drive superior results?

Financial performance is the bottom line for proving the case for Dare-to-Serve Leadership—and we have delivered the goods. Perhaps nothing is more compelling

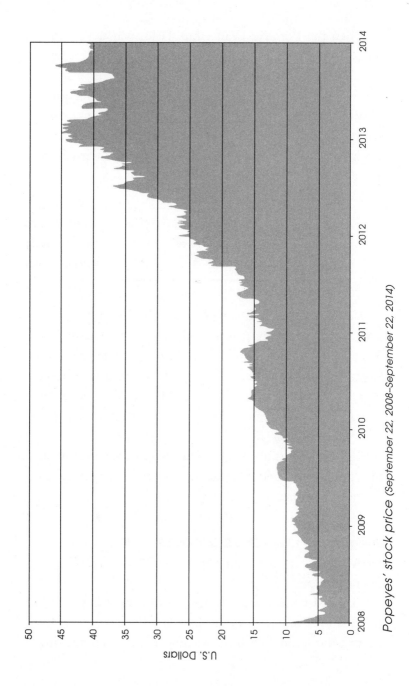

Popeyes' stock price (September 22, 2008–September 22, 2014)

than our share price performance. From September 2008 to September 2014, the Popeyes share price grew from below $10 to above $40, as indicated in the chart. The stock has also outpaced the S&P 500 restaurant sector and the total S&P 500 in this timeframe.

Wall Street, take note. While a compelling business strategy is essential, the principles that guide *how* leaders accomplish that plan will determine the trajectory of the results.

Principles perform.

PART TWO

HOW TO BECOME A
DARE-TO-SERVE LEADER

Everyone thinks of changing humanity,
and nobody thinks of changing himself.
LEO TOLSTOY

I worked many years in large corporations *without ever thinking about my work as "service to others." Early in my career, when people asked me my career philosophy, I would say, "Think like a man, act like a lady, and work like a dog." I took this line from the cover of a book I had never read, yet I quoted the title for twenty years.*

Did I seek the spotlight? You bet.

Like many, I experienced success: achieving results, getting rewarded, and being promoted. Because my field was marketing and innovation, I enjoyed coming up with bold, daring ideas to grow the business. I enjoyed getting work done in teams. I had plenty of courage, but I'm not sure I had true humility. I did not know that a leader who stepped out of the spotlight to serve others would drive superior performance results. I certainly had not seen a demonstration.

Along the way, I met leaders in nonprofit organizations who were definitely serving others. They ran soup kitchens and homes for abused women. They were missionaries and social workers. I admired their leadership and the profound impact they had on other people's lives. In retrospect, I was probably embarrassed to compare leadership in for-profit companies to this more noble work.

In contrast, my bosses in for-profit organizations were usually focused on getting more of the spotlight for themselves. In fact, most made the spotlight their number-one priority. The work environment these leaders created did not lift up and celebrate others. Often, the business results were mediocre.

Puzzled by the apparent courage in some leaders and the humility in others, I reflected on what kind of leader I wanted to be.

Conclusion?

The leader must have both—the courage to take the people to a daring destination and the humility to selflessly serve others on the journey. This dynamic tension between daring and serving creates the conditions for superior performance.

I wish I'd figured this out sooner.

CHOOSE TO SERVE

Do nothing from selfish ambition or conceit, but in
humility count others more significant than yourselves.

PHILIPPIANS 2:3

IN MY VERY FIRST JOB OUT OF COLLEGE, I was in a meeting in the corner office with the guy everyone called "the
big boss." The meeting was to make an important decision on the business. As we huddled around his conference table, he pondered the facts and said to us, "We
need to do an end run."

I had no idea what he was talking about, so my eyes
quickly and carefully darted around the room to see how
others would react. Would we jump up and run? Would
we duck for cover? Thankfully, all that happened was
that we picked up our papers and went back to our desks.

I needed some training in football terms. I also needed
lessons in leadership.

From that day forward I have been trying to figure out
leadership—what is it? what are the traits of a leader?—
especially leaders who drive superior performance results.

The first place I looked for clues? I studied my bosses.

BOSS OBSERVATIONS

*I've never known a person who didn't light up at the memory
of a truly great boss. And for good reason—they can shape
and advance your career in ways you never expected—
and sometimes they can even change your life.*
In stark contrast, a bad boss can just about kill you.

JACK WELCH, *WINNING*

About halfway through my career, I worked for two dramatically different kinds of bosses back-to-back. It was
easy to compare them, as I worked for the first boss for
one year, followed by one year working for the next boss.

I'll never forget my initial meeting with that first boss.
When I came to his office, his words to me were, "I chose
you for this role. Your talent is just what we need. I look
forward to working with you. This is going to be fun."
This was a welcome like no other. He was genuinely enthusiastic to have me on his team. I remember thinking
that I'd never had a conversation like that before.

For the next year with that first boss, I led a brand-
building team that was charged with creating a pipeline
of innovative new products. I was supervising the largest
group of people of my career thus far. It was a stretch
assignment. At home, I was a wife and mother, juggling
the demands of family. Life was complicated, but good.

The first boss was interested in all of that. He partici-
pated in our new product ideation sessions, encouraging
us to be bold and creative. He invested his time in our
development as leaders, offering words of wisdom that
would shape us for years to come. He seemed to enjoy knowing about our life outside of work—he even

had a nickname for my daughter ("Blue Shoes"). During his tenure, our performance results soared. We were the best-performing business unit in the company—and we loved our jobs.

I remember just as clearly the arrival of my second boss. It happened in the second year. He was introduced at a large company-wide meeting. He gave a speech and said he was excited to be promoted. He had big ambitions.

This boss invited me out for dinner—a "get to know you" opportunity. Somewhere during that dinner, he said these words, "I've heard you are good. My job is to trip you up." Then he grinned—as if that were a funny thing to say. I've never forgotten those words.

Those words proved to be the second boss's worldview—find people's faults and errors. Make sure that the people know the boss is smarter and better than they are in every respect. Because the boss is "going places" in the company.

The second boss also decided to invest in my personal development as a leader. He hired an industrial psychologist named Frank who gave me a series of tests and wrote an eighteen-page report on my personality and opportunities for improvement. My report concluded that I did not read the *Wall Street Journal* enough and my suits needed an upgrade. I remember that day pretty clearly, too.

A year later, under the leadership of the second boss, this company had lost momentum and most of its leaders had left, including me. A couple years after that, the business was sold to another company.

What did I learn from the contrast of my first and second bosses?

The first boss served the people extremely well, but he was no milquetoast either. He challenged us to pursue bold ideas. He spoke to us with encouraging words that made his confidence in us clear. He also had big aspirations—for the people and for the enterprise. Under his leadership, we accomplished superior performance results. It was one of the best experiences of my career.

DARE-TO-SERVE REFLECTION #22 *Who was your best boss? Who was your worst boss? Which one led you to your best performance results? Why?*

The second boss was plenty smart. He challenged us to do HIS ideas. He spoke to us with condescending words that made it clear he thought we were less capable than he was. He had big ambitions—for his own career. And the performance results tanked. It was one of the worst experiences of my career, and I quit as soon as possible.

This experience was a turning point in my views on leadership. I decided that I wanted to be like Boss No. 1—"for the people." With equal zeal, I decided that I must avoid at all costs the behaviors of Boss No. 2 that killed the energy of the team and led to the end of a top-performing organization.

STUDY OF LEADERSHIP

I began studying different approaches to leadership.

Robert Greenleaf introduced this concept of the servant leader in the late 1970s—*one who leads by putting the well-being of others first.*

Greenleaf was not a professor or a researcher. He was a middle manager in one of the twentieth century's largest organizations, AT&T. He was a thoughtful, optimistic kind of guy, who had observed leaders in real-world situations. I think that is why I liked his views. They seemed based on reality.

In his writing, Greenleaf concluded that, at the extremes, a leader chooses to be either Leader First or Servant First—a leader who focuses on self-ambition, or a leader whose ambition is to serve others.

The Leader First motto could be "it's all about me": self-focused leadership. This leader seeks a position of power, enjoys getting and wielding power, and seeks to win for personal gain. These leaders have an integrity filter that is selective, meaning they do what is right, as long as it serves them well.

The Servant First motto could well be "it's all about the people": others-focused leadership. This leader is in a position of power, but uses the position to share power—listening to people, collaborating with people, and seeking a win for the people and the enterprise. These leaders have moral integrity as their filter. They do what is right, no matter what the cost to self.

Greenleaf said few leaders are actually at the extremes—either 100 percent Leader First or 100 percent Servant First.

After more than thirty-five years of my own observations, I don't think there are "bad guy" leaders and "good guy" leaders—we all have bad and good traits. The problem is, we fail to deliberately decide between the two poles of self-serving leadership and serving others well.

We wobble back and forth between serving the people well and serving our own interests. In fact, we wobble from day to day and hour to hour. We lack conviction. *We struggle between who we are and who we wish we could be.*

DARE-TO-SERVE REFLECTION #23 *How would your daily behaviors be different if you put them through a filter of serving others well?*

REFLECTIONS ON REALITY

I'm amused by the recent spate of reality shows about business and leadership. They reflect our cultural norms about how leaders accomplish great results.

In 2004, NBC launched *The Apprentice*, with Donald Trump, the billionaire real-estate mogul, pitting two teams against each other until one candidate earns the privilege of a job with The Trump Organization. It quickly became the number-one new show on television. In addition to the manipulative and cutthroat behaviors that make good television, its legacy has been two words: *"You're fired."*

In 2009, ABC launched *Shark Tank*, in which tough, self-made multimillionaires give budding entrepreneurs a chance to secure funding for their business ideas. It is the American version of a global show called *Dragons' Den*. In each episode, the "sharks" confront the flaws in an entrepreneur's concept—and we watch as dreams are slayed by dragons. Sharks and dragons leave a clear picture in our minds about business leadership.

These may be our favorite television shows—but do they represent the leaders you want to work for? If not, then we must consider an alternative approach.

Would you be willing to lead differently, to serve others, if it produced superior results?

If so, you will need to avoid these traps.

Serving Trap No. 1: Power I once produced a musical. That's actually not as impressive as it might sound, because at the time I was nine years old, at a family reunion.

Even though I was only a kid, I was the oldest child in the group. I decided to name myself as producer and boss. I would pick the play we'd perform and I would assign parts to each of the cousins.

It was 1965 and my favorite movie that year was *The Sound of Music.*

Naturally, *I* was going to sing the title song so I assigned myself the lead. To help me "get into" my role, I snuck into my mother's closet and pulled out, as my costume, her wedding dress. All my cousins got lesser roles.

I'm not sure my performance brought tears to the eyes of the adults who had to sit through the play. This I am sure of. At nine years old, I was a power leader. I wielded my power over others to accomplish my desired result. It was "all about me." My cousins remind me of this to this day.

Every leadership position comes with some degree of power. The question is, how will a leader use the power they have been given?

Leveraging power over others is the primary leadership model celebrated in our culture. We celebrate leaders chasing power, getting power, and wielding power over others. This is what leaders do—or so we think.

We celebrate the trappings of power. Title. Status. Money. Education. Anything that makes it clear that the leader is better than the rest of the people.

Is power a problem only for CEOs? No. All leaders are at risk of grabbing power for their own purposes.

DARE-TO-SERVE REFLECTION #24 *How do you use the power that comes with your position: for personal gain or for serving the people and the enterprise?*

Have you noticed the behaviors of a newly promoted boss in your organization? Do they suddenly act "in charge"? Do they become stern, hands on hips, with a much louder voice? Do they wear the power on their sleeve?

Power over others, the authority you have been given, will be the driver of your leadership unless you make a conscious decision otherwise. Will you use your power for serving others?

Serving Trap No. 2: Achievement In my sophomore year of high school, my family moved to Cupertino, California, where I attended Monta Vista High School. This was an academically challenging school, and I had to step up my game. At the first parents' night, my dad was embarrassed to see that I had not yet passed any of the quizzes in Algebra II/Trigonometry. He let me know that I was grounded until I caught up in math class.

It was a good decision to ground me. I quickly figured out that I needed to study more to get good grades. My dad also provided an incentive—telling me that he would take me out for a fine steak dinner when I received straight As on my report card.

In the spring of my junior year, I achieved the goal of straight As. I made myself a long, pink "maxi" dress and my dad took me out for a steak dinner at a famous restaurant in San Francisco.

At the age of seventeen, I discovered "personal achievement" and it felt good. But it was "all about me." There are still days when I find myself chasing straight "As" and missing the opportunity to serve.

My learning about achievement came from school. Yours may have come from sports or some other form of competition. Wherever you learned achievement, the idea is deeply rooted in your being. Winning is good. Losing is bad.

DARE-TO-SERVE REFLECTION #25 *What is the most important achievement of your life? Was the win for you—or for the people on your team?*

There would be no movie named *Chariots of Fire* if Eric Liddell had not won his 400-meter race in the 1924 Olympics. We would not remember Alexander the Great if he had not conquered the Persian Empire. Bill Gates, founder of Microsoft, would not be celebrated if his venture had gone bankrupt.

There are no great leaders without great achievements. Achievement is an essential aspect of leadership.

The critical question: *Is the achievement for you or for the people?*

What is your view of achievement? What are you worrying about—your promotion, your next raise, getting recognition, moving to a bigger office?

Your answer?

Serving Trap No. 3: Ambition Upon graduating from college, I started my first job at Procter & Gamble in Cincinnati, Ohio. My field was called brand management. There was an entering class of sixty new hires that fall—young college and business school graduates seeking success. I quickly observed that the first big marker in our brand management career was how fast we could reach field sales training. This three-month assignment was required for our first promotion. The sixty of us began to chase that goal to see who would get there first.

I began to learn about ambition. Ambition gave me focus on the future—a goal to shoot for. Work seemed to be measured in salary raises and promotions. My ambition was to reach these milestones and gain the recognition that went with promotions. I had discovered ambition and I liked it, yet it was "all about me."

Ambition is a cultural norm for leadership. Defined by Merriam-Webster as "an ardent desire for rank, fame, or power," the word comes from the Latin word *ambitio*, literally the act of soliciting votes for political office. In these roots, we find the problem with ambition. Ambition is a problem if it is all about you.

What would ambition be if it were for the benefit of the people and the enterprise? Perhaps a better word is an *aspiration* for the people we serve?

The definition of aspiration is "a strong desire to achieve something high or great."

Is it all about your ambition, or could we *aspire* to achieve something great together?

DARE-TO-SERVE REFLECTION #26 *Do you have big ambitions for yourself or big aspirations for the people on your team?*

YOUR CHOICE: SPOTLIGHT OR DARE TO SERVE?

What can we conclude about leaders who love the spotlight on themselves? Self-centered leadership is the enemy of high-performing teams.

- It doesn't develop the talents of the people and squashes their desire to take risks.

- It may hold people accountable, but does so without supportive coaching to drive performance.

- It relies on authority, because there are no genuine relationships for influence.

- It is overly confident, without a sound sense of reality—because the followers have stopped talking to the leader.

Self-centered leadership is actually a *lazy* path. The leader merely wields power over others to achieve results for their own benefit. This is not difficult to do. But this approach stunts the performance of the people and the enterprise. It *cannot* deliver superior results.

Dare-to-Serve Leadership is much more difficult, and in that challenge, the leader creates the conditions for superior performance:

- It begins with a conscious and humble decision to serve others well.

- It inspires people to pursue a daring destination, an aspiration greater than self.

- It boosts the capability of the people and increases their willingness to take risks.

- It holds people accountable.

- It is appropriately confident.

- It works.

Dare-to-Serve Leadership requires deep-rooted personal conviction; it's a demanding path.

The Dare-to-Serve Leader has that unique combination of traits—enough courage to take the team to a daring destination, and enough humility to serve the people well on the journey. Together these traits foster the environment for superior performance.

Will you make this more difficult and demanding choice?

Will you choose to serve?

SIX

BE **BOLD** AND **BRAVE**

I learned that courage was not the absence of fear,
but the triumph over it. The brave man is not he who
does not feel afraid, but he who conquers that fear.

NELSON MANDELA

A FRIEND OF MINE went bungee jumping in South Africa—jumping off the Bloukrans Bridge, plunging over a spectacular gorge. Rising 709 feet over the Bloukrans River, the bridge is the world's highest commercial bungee jump location (though it is only the thirty-sixth highest bridge in the world). The local operator of this extreme sport has appropriately named his company Face Adrenalin.

When my friend got home from the trip, she showed me the videotape of her jump. During the several minutes of preparation for the jump, while the guides secured her in the harness, my friend screamed and cried as though she was going to die any minute.

I completely relate to that emotion—I probably would have died of fear on the platform. Being much braver than I, my friend made the jump and found herself swinging upside down over Bloukrans River until the crew pulled her back up to the top. She told me how amazing the experience was—how it felt to fly through the air with the blood rushing into her head.

Being averse to physical risk-taking, this idea of bungee jumping makes absolutely no sense to me. In fact, it seems outright crazy. So why do people take this kind of risk—and what benefits do they get from the experience?

In 2009, Eric Brymer and Lindsay Oades published research on the mindset and effects of participation in extreme sports. Their findings may surprise you. In the people they interviewed, who pursue sports like BASE jumping, waterfall kayaking, big wave surfing, and extreme mountaineering, the researchers discovered a positive transformation in the *courage and humility* of the participants. Apparently pursuing activities that involve a real chance of death transforms us in a positive way, increasing our courage for risk taking while humbling us as we realize we do not control the outcomes.

Dare-to-Serve Leadership reflects this same paradox.

It requires immense courage and a deeply humble soul at the same time. The leader must call out a daring aspiration for the people—bold enough to risk failure. The leader must give the people confidence that the destination can be reached, yet humbly accept that they do not control all the outcomes. This tension of the uncertain outcome, combined with the leader's commitment to help the people reach the destination, yields the exciting performance results. Leading is an extreme sport.

LEADERS ARE BOLD

Great leaders have bold ideas—their aspirations for the people are big. Think about leaders in history. Are there any you remember as great who had *small* aspirations for the people?

Gandhi? Mother Teresa? Martin Luther King, Jr.?

Even leaders with bad ideas are remembered for their boldness. Hitler? Stalin? Mao?

My first close-up study of daring aspirations in business leadership took place while I was working for Domino's Pizza founder Tom Monaghan. I worked for Tom from 1995 until he sold the company in 1998 to Bain Capital. I had never been that close to a successful entrepreneur—it was better than any MBA class I ever took.

I once asked Tom what his original aspiration was when he first started the company. It was a daring destination. He said, "I thought I would have one Domino's in every college town in America, which at that time would have been about two hundred." Tom's only other property at this early stage of life was a Volkswagen Beetle, which he owned with his brother, yet he was dreaming big. His bold idea attracted entrepreneurs to Domino's who wanted to be part of making history happen.

Tom's career was a steady stream of bold actions.

Tom was boldly innovative. He once told me that he wasn't much of a marketer. Yet I had already heard the story of how at the first store he was hanging Domino's coupons on apartment doors. He marked each coupon with a code number. When a customer purchased a pizza with a coupon, Tom would tally the redemption rates. Tom had no marketing training, but he essentially invented direct marketing years before it came into vogue. Franchise owners used this method to grow Domino's Pizza sales for years to come.

Tom was bold in charitable giving. He was well known as a devout Catholic, one of the largest donors in the church. It was not unusual to see Cardinal Maida visiting Tom's office in red robes, or to see Tom take a call from the Vatican to handle a request to buy a jeep for nuns in Central America. Tom was bold in giving help to those in need.

DARE-TO-SERVE REFLECTION #27 *How will your daring aspiration for the organization grow the capability and experience of the team?*

Tom was bold with his values at work. He would admit that in many ways he fell short in living his values, but he urged Domino's leaders to always aim high. Some of Tom's values were the conventional ones—such as honesty in every action. Some values took a more subtle form—such as paying the company bills immediately. Tom directed the Chief Financial Officer (CFO) to pay Domino's bills when they arrived, not using the standard cash payment terms. He didn't think it was right to use the supplier's cash to his advantage. Despite the CFO's pleading, Tom held his ground.

Tom's bold vision to build two hundred Domino's was accomplished in 1978. But by the time he sold the company to Bain Capital in 1998, there were over 6,000 stores, 1,500 of them outside of the United States. More than 1,000 Domino's franchisees were in business as a result of Tom's big idea. The people were served well.

The daring leader helps the people see a future state that is greater than their own imagination and worthy of pursuit. By pursuing a bold aspiration, the people grow in capability and experience—stretching to accomplish things they never dreamed of.

The leader who serves the people well provides a daring aspiration to the organization.

WHAT DARING DESTINATION COULD YOU PURSUE?

As I look back on my early working life, I think my first daring aspiration for the people and the enterprise occurred while working on the Life Savers candy business. (Yes, believe it or not, there is a job growing the Life Savers candy business.) At the time, Life Savers were used largely by grandmothers to keep children quiet at church. It was not a vibrant, growth business.

While I was working on this relatively low-level problem in the 1980s, the president of the United States was thinking about how to prevent missile attacks from other countries, particularly from the Soviet Union. President Reagan set forth a daring aspiration for the nation—it was called the Strategic Defense Initiative (SDI). The idea was that the United States could develop a sophisticated anti–ballistic missile system that would use lasers to shoot down missiles in midair before they reached land.

I remember thinking SDI was a bold, aspirational idea. When it was time to present my bold new ambition for the future of the Life Savers brand, I flew to Norfolk, Virginia, to make a presentation to the senior executives. How did I keep the attention of my audience? I called my presentation the "Life Savers Strategic Defense Initiative."

Inside the presentation, I put the team's boldest ideas for rejuvenating the Life Savers brand. There were three: a new candy called Life Savers Fruit Juicers with 10 percent real fruit juice; a new candy called Life Savers Holes (imagine the dot missing in the center of a Life Saver); and the first U.S. gummi candy in the shape of a Life Saver—Life Savers Gummi Savers.

Our Life Savers SDI plan did not execute perfectly, but in the end it had good performance statistics.

Life Savers Fruit Juicers played on a trend of the times—adding 10 percent fruit juice to everything in the grocery store. Moms felt better giving their children candy with real fruit juice and sales and market share increased nicely. Fruit Juicers eventually ran out of steam, but for a time, it rejuvenated the brand.

Life Savers Holes was complicated. Despite the imaginary idea that every Life Savers candy produced a "hole" with no place to go, the truth was we had to engineer equipment to make hard candy in this very small "hole" format. Then we had to create a plastic package to hold the "holes." Both the candy and packaging equipment were expensive. There was a very tiny bit of candy in an expensive plastic container. Life Savers Holes was launched with much fanfare and excitement, but ended up as a short-lived fad that fell way short of the returns we promised.

Finally, we hit the home-run idea. Life Savers Gummi Savers was a tender, chewy gummi candy with the amazing flavors you loved in a Life Saver. The only competitors at the time were tough, stale gummi bears imported from Europe. We produced an award-winning advertisement of these squishy candies doing a conga-line dance—showing off their tenderness and flavor. The ad won trophies but, more importantly, the business delivered $100 million in new candy sales.

The Life Savers "SDI" presentation was boldly ambitious—some would say "crazy." Yet it put forth three fresh, innovative ideas; while they didn't all work well or last forever, these new products gave the team new capabilities, new experiences, and new confidence. For the corporation, they delivered sales and profit growth.

DARE-TO-SERVE REFLECTION #28 *Think about a bold initiative that you have been a part of. How did it prepare you well for future leadership?*

At first blush, you might consider it silly to think that a new candy could be called a courageous act that served the people well. I challenge you to think about the effect on the people of this bold ambition. The greatest legacy of this work was the impact of the performance results on the people:

- Engineers created innovative new ways to manufacture candy—growing skills and confidence.

- Manufacturing plants were expanded to make the new products—adding new jobs for people in the community.

- Leaders were promoted to new responsibilities.

- Leaders learned invaluable lessons from the mistakes and failures.

- A brand, Life Savers, was renewed—and serves its customers well to this day.

HOW BRAVE?

Just how brave should your bold idea be? I'm probably not the right person to ask.

One of the bravest ideas ever presented to me was a new invention for keeping pizzas hot. The prototype looked like a sixth-grade science project—complete with visible wires and duct tape holding it together. You needed a lot of imagination to see this as a real possibility.

The invention was a heated disk that, when inserted in a pizza delivery bag, would keep the pizza oven-hot until it reached your front door. When the delivery driver returned to the store, he or she plugged the disk into the wall—and it reheated for the next delivery.

The inventor believed that keeping the pizza at the same temperature that it exited the oven—all the way to your home—would be a compelling competitive advantage.

I agreed with him. And my job responsibility at the time was to lead Marketing and Innovation at Domino's Pizza. Here was my crazy thought . . .

Domino's had invented the 30-minute delivered pizza —pizza delivered in 30 minutes or it was free. A complicated lawsuit had resulted in the end of that famous 30-minute guarantee.

Domino's also had a lagging quality reputation—people described it as "the cardboard-tasting pizza I ate in college." Not a compelling reason to buy.

We had just invested in a product improvement to make the crust taste better, but we didn't have a bold new idea to replace the loss of the famous 30-minutes-or-free guarantee.

When I saw the sixth-grade science project prototype, I believed we had discovered the answer. Boldly, I presented the heated delivery bag to the executives of Domino's as our next big innovation—explaining the temperature advantage that we could market against competitors . . . and the advantage of keeping our new, improved pizzas oven-hot all the way to your door.

My peers were now certain that I had lost my mind.

The supply-chain executive was concerned about how this equipment would be manufactured and what its failure rate would be. The operations executive thought it was too complicated to handle in the restaurants. The finance executive could not believe that there would be a return on this investment. The franchisee executive was sure that the franchise owners would balk at the capital required to buy this equipment.

DARE-TO-SERVE REFLECTION #29 *What prevents you from pursuing a daring aspiration for the organization? Do you worry that others may think the plan is crazy? Do you have anxiety that you might fail?*

I presented this bold idea seven times to the executive team and CEO, Tom Monaghan.

Seven times they rejected the idea, for a whole lot of good reasons.

In a short private conversation with Tom Monaghan, we landed on the question we had to answer as a team: "How will we feel on the day that Pizza Hut is the first to launch heated delivery bags with superior taste and temperature? And what will our franchise owners say then?"

Tom, the daring entrepreneur, answered the question

with, "We're going to launch the heated delivery bag—and we're going to be first."

The Domino's HeatWave bag was born that day and launched nationwide several months after that. The technology WAS new and imperfect. The launch had bumps and costs that many of my peers had forecast. But the bold decision Tom made to launch the HeatWave bag drove sales and market share for the next five years. To this day, it is a competitive advantage that serves the owners and customers of Domino's Pizza well.

GO BIG OR GO HOME

I have a weird personality. I only want to work on big, huge, hard things. Maybe it is my wiring of being an idea person. Maybe it is my love of turnaround opportunities. Maybe it reflects my total lack of patience for slow-moving endeavors.

This I am certain of: I want to work on something that matters. I want to either go big or go home.

On that point, I don't think I'm the only one. I think the people whom we lead want to work on something that matters. I think the people would rather try something bold and exciting and fail, than never be challenged.

It is the responsibility of the leader to have a daring aspiration for the people and the enterprise. If we don't, the people will not be well served. But I should probably warn you, bold, brave leaders don't win popularity contests.

In business, the bold leaders are described by many as quirky, strange, and even a bit loony. People will say you lack practical knowledge; you will probably blow the budget; and many other unattractive things. People always have handy the five reasons your idea will fail in the "real" world. People will accuse you of fiscal irresponsibility. The road to bold thinking is paved with doubters and naysayers.

The "cheers" don't come until the daring idea transforms the organization, rejuvenates a tired brand, or turns around a poorly performing team. Then everyone will cheer the bold idea that saved the day.

If you are a bold leader, with big aspirations for the people and the enterprise, bring your courage and confidence—or your ideas will never leave the paper they are written on.

DARE-TO-SERVE REFLECTION #30 *What is your daring aspiration for your team that is beyond what they know how to accomplish today?*

At the beginning of this chapter, I suggested that pursuing risky activities that involve a real chance of death transforms people in a positive way. The experience builds our courage while humbling us, as we realize we do not control the outcomes.

If you choose to have a daring aspiration for the people and the enterprise, you will step out in courage—and you will be humbled by lessons learned along the way.

Dare-to-Serve Leadership is transformative for the leader *and* the followers. In taking a risk, the leader *and* the people stretch and grow—and when successful, they experience new confidence and new commitment to the team. They are winners, but humbly realize that the win would have been impossible by themselves.

Be a bold and brave leader. Serve the people well.

SEVEN

HAVE **CLARITY** OF **PURPOSE**

ABOUT TEN YEARS AGO, I developed a bit of an obsession. I started asking this question of everyone I met: "Why do you work?"

I could see them trying to figure out what answer I was looking for. Because that is what we do when we are asked a question—we try to give the right answer.

So they would try to stay calm and say the expected: "I work to put my kids through college." "I work to pay the bills." "I work to support my mother."

These were appropriate responses, even noble.

But the answers gradually reveal that the person doesn't have an answer to the question.

Awkward silence. I could sense them thinking, *What if there is no purpose for my work? What if work is meaningless?*

So I'd change the subject . . . "How was your week-end?"

I finally met someone who wasn't stumped by the question, "Why do you work?"

That someone is Chris. He is my hairdresser.

Chris welcomes me to his chair. He is immensely interested in my day. He offers a neck massage, asks how my haircut is working, and wonders if there is anything about it I want to change? For forty-five minutes, the stressful world evaporates as Chris and I banter. I'm feeling better already. I tease him that I wish I could stop by every day.

When I asked Chris, "Why do you work?" he responded:

> In my twenties I was a partier. I didn't go to college. I didn't have a career plan. I was enjoying life—playing sports and hanging out with buddies.
>
> My parents kept asking me about my plan, but I wasn't too concerned. Then I met this girl I really liked, and she wanted to know my plan. I decided I better get one.
>
> A friend suggested I go to beauty school and make a living cutting hair.
>
> At beauty school, I found I had talent. With training, my skills improved. I discovered that what I loved about the job was this . . .
>
> A woman would sit in my chair—usually stressed, feeling bad about how she looked. She needed encouragement. To face another day, she needed to be renewed.
>
> I started making her renewal my purpose. I saw how she relaxed after a neck massage. I saw how she appreciated me shampooing her hair. I saw how she started to open up and tell me about her life. I found opportunities to tell her she was interesting to talk to. I worked hard to get her hair styled just right—whether she was going out on an important date or not. When she left my chair, I wanted her to feel differently about herself.
>
> Every day I get the opportunity to lift up women— encouraging them, making them feel beautiful. They leave my chair with confidence—a spring in their step. That is so much fun to watch.

Chris knows exactly what he is doing at work. He knows why he is a hairdresser. He has a purpose.

This purpose has served his clients well—and it has served Chris well. Chris is a top-producing hairdresser in one of the most popular salons in Atlanta. He is booked solid from morning till night and his tips are huge. He is making good money and living a meaningful life.

DARE-TO-SERVE REFLECTION #31   *Why do you work? Do you have a purpose beyond paying the bills?*

Most hairdressers work every Saturday, some Sundays, and the night before every holiday. Chris doesn't. He only works Monday through Friday, a normal work-week, with a back-to-back schedule of women who will wait days just to see Chris.

He serves. He has purpose. He has superior performance results.

PURSUING CLARITY OF PURPOSE

Before you can help others find their purpose at work, you must find your own. The process is no different for you than the team process described in chapter 3. But heed this warning: it is much harder to find clarity in your own personal purpose than to help others find theirs.

Some say that your purpose is easier to identify when you are old. Others say it is easier when you are young. My observation is that, no matter what your age or experience, finding clarity in your personal purpose is just plain hard. It requires honest self-evaluation. It requires a certain transparency to share with others. And, worst of all, it makes us feel vulnerable in front of people—a feeling we find miserable.

My advice? Push through all these barriers to reach clarity of personal purpose. The benefits far outweigh the risks.

EXAMINE YOUR LIFE

I've come to believe that every life has a theme. Sometimes it takes a long time to discover our theme, but if we pause and look back over time, the pattern presents itself in the stories of our lives.

For me personally, leadership is my life theme. You can hear it in the stories of my life.

DARE-TO-SERVE REFLECTION #32 *Looking back over your life, what themes reoccur? How can you use those experiences to positively impact your team?*

It began with the leaders in my family, grandparents and parents who spoke the lessons of leadership into my life. Leadership skills learned while organizing game night at family reunions. Leadership lessons learned by listening to my dad's stories. Leadership experienced as the oldest of four children.

In the workplace, leadership developed as I moved through positions at Procter & Gamble, the Gillette Company, and RJR Nabisco. Leadership lessons gained from working with an iconic entrepreneur, Tom Monaghan.

Leadership refined by the joys and trials of life as a parent of three children.

Until we stop and reflect on our lifeline, we miss the

themes of life experience, themes that could guide us to a clear purpose for our roles as leaders.

Look back over your life experiences and determine the consistent themes that you see in the timeline.

CHOOSE YOUR VALUES

I've yet to meet anyone who says, "I have no values." At the same time, I've rarely met anyone who can tell me what their values are—and how they impact their daily work.

What are your values?

Most people will quickly list a few noble values. But if I asked you this question, you might have to pause and think: Are those the values that you use to organize the decisions and activities in your workday? Or are your values less active in your daily work? Do they sit in the background, as aspirations that you hope over time will prove true?

To serve others at work, we need to put more thought into the values that govern our day.

DARE-TO-SERVE REFLECTION #33 *How will your top-priority values contribute to the performance of your team and organization? How do you want to be remembered?*

There are numerous exercises for reaching a better understanding of your values. As mentioned in chapter 3, a simple tool is a deck of cards from the John Maxwell organization, thirty-four values, each defined on a card, which makes it easy for you to sort out the ones that are most important to you.

Your task: decide which *three* values you want to be evident to the people at work. Three values that you want others to hold you accountable to. Three values that you will be remembered for on the day you leave the organization.

For me personally, after faith and family, the top three values that influence my leadership are:

- Legacy—I want to make a difference in the lives of the people I lead.

- Integrity—I want my daily actions to match my core values.

- Learning—I never want to stop growing and learning new things.

These are not the only values—nor the "best" values. They are simply the three values that I want to be evident in my leadership.

What will yours be?

KNOW YOUR GIFTS

Finding your purpose for work begins with the inner journey of discovering your innate strengths and talents. My hairdresser, Chris, found he was gifted in cutting hair. You may be gifted in teaching, in innovative thinking, caring for others' needs, or providing wise counsel.

A landmark book called *Now, Discover Your Strengths* by Marcus Buckingham and Donald O. Clifton establishes this premise: you have strengths—find them and put them to work to best serve your team and your organization.

Your workplace typically doesn't talk to you about

your strengths. In fact, the traditional annual performance review is usually an hour-long conversation about your weaknesses, euphemistically described as your "opportunities for improvement." This is discouraging and distracting feedback.

DARE-TO-SERVE REFLECTION #34 *What are your best talents that you can offer to the organization? Are you using those talents in your current role?*

At a presentation some years ago on this topic, I heard this statement, "You can spend your whole life working on improving your weaknesses, and gain only a 15 percent improvement." I can't remember the speaker's name, but I've never forgotten the words.

The speaker continued, saying, "Spend your life applying your strengths, and your contributions will grow exponentially."

This is a life-changing concept at work. To know why you work, you must discover your unique strengths and then spend the rest of your working days offering those strengths to your employer. That is what you are designed to do. Any other path will be frustrating and difficult.

There are numerous talent assessments that can help you discover your most important strengths—StrengthsFinder and StandOut are two of my favorites. For $10 or $15 you can do these assessments online and within minutes have clarity about your top five strengths or your top two StandOut roles. I recommend you do this today.

Know your talents and offer them to your organization.

WRITE YOUR PURPOSE

As you increase your understanding of your life experiences, your values, and your strengths, you have an opportunity to bring these lessons together in a statement of your personal purpose.

Your personal purpose is one or two sentences that capture the essence of who you are and how you will serve others. Here are a few examples:

- "To build a sense of community in my team that makes work meaningful and fun."

- "To serve as a trusted advisor wherever I can add value."

- "To give others a sense of dignity—to know that their life matters."

- "To teach others to creatively solve problems that others run from."

When you land on your personal purpose, you will have a good reason for going to work each day—a good reason for the time you invest leading others. When you know your purpose, you will have a way to evaluate whether you are doing what matters most. Without purpose, you will struggle to see any meaning in what you do. The job will simply be a paycheck.

Here's the most important point. If you have no purpose for serving others at work—they will know. *The people know your motive whether you know it or not.*

A leader without a personal purpose is leading the people on a pointless, meaningless journey. And that's exactly the environment your leadership creates. A meaningless journey . . .

Is that what you want your leadership legacy to be? Only you can change that outcome for the people you lead. Only you can decide your personal purpose for serving others well.

DARE-TO-SERVE REFLECTION #35 *When will you set aside time to reach clarity about your personal purpose for serving others?*

The Journey to Personal Purpose exercise is available at www.daretoserveleaders.com. The one-page format is shown in chapter 3 (see Journey to Personal Purpose Exercise 4).

TEST YOUR PURPOSE

Many have asked me how to make sure their purpose is "true." Out of those discussions came this list of ways to test the genuineness, the authenticity of your personal purpose:

Authenticity Test: Find a person who knows you well and tell them your lifeline, your values, your talents, and your purpose. Ask them if this rings true to who you are. Is this the authentic you?

Others Test: Ask yourself, "If I lead like this, will the people I lead be better off?" Leadership is about how you serve others. If your purpose is only about you, revise it.

Action Test: Ask yourself, "Now that I have this statement, what exactly will I do differently to make it evident to those I lead?" If you can't determine at least three specific action steps you will take as a result of your purpose, go back and edit it to be so clear and specific that it will drive you to clear action steps.

Hundred Day Test: Implement your personal purpose action steps for one hundred days. Then stop and reflect on your purpose. Is it accurate? Is it authentically you? Are there subtle changes you want to make? Edit and try for another one hundred days.

Of these tests, the most important is the Action Test. For your personal purpose to have an impact on the lives of others, you have to put it to work in your daily life. Organize your calendar with the filter of your purpose. At the end of your day or week, ask yourself, "Did I live my purpose this week? What examples could I give? Did I miss opportunities because I was busy or distracted with other things?"

THE POINT OF PURPOSE

It's not about you.

RICK WARREN, *THE PURPOSE DRIVEN LIFE*

I understand where you might be today. I have been a leader without a personal purpose. I led teams for decades without a clear purpose for serving others well.

Then, while going through a time of struggle and reflection, I read a book called *The Purpose Driven Life*. The first paragraph reminded me that when you are asked to be a leader, it is for the sake of others; it is not about you —and this changed my approach to leadership forever.

The point of purpose is to determine how you will serve others. If you don't plan to serve, you don't need a purpose.

If you do choose to serve, a personal purpose will determine the focus of your leadership.

In my current role, I have concluded that my personal purpose is: *To inspire purpose-driven leaders to exhibit competence and character in all aspects of their life.*

This personal purpose is the filter I now use for determining how I spend my time in leadership and work. Here are just a few of the ways my focus has shifted.

- Mondays and Tuesdays of every week are now dedicated to one-on-one coaching sessions with Popeyes leaders, my direct reports.

- Every six months I choose one vice president– level leader to mentor with six 90-minute sessions on any topics they choose.

- My restaurant tours are now focused on getting to know the restaurant's general manager and finding out how our company can better serve them.

- When asked to speak at public events, I only speak on the topic of leadership.

Purpose has helped me decide what to say yes to. Purpose has helped me decide what to say no to.

I enjoy my work more than ever, because I'm doing what I care most about. I also feel my life has more significance because I am singularly focused on how I want to make a difference in the lives of others.

Purpose has led me to develop deeper, richer relationships at work. Like you, I spend the majority of my waking hours at work. Being intentional about developing future leaders has given me the opportunity to build meaningful relationships with Popeyes leaders and franchise owners.

For me, the most startling outcome of personal purpose is how it has changed my performance as a leader. The performance results of Popeyes are by far the most impressive outcomes I have been associated with in my career. I am humbled to realize how long it took me to learn this lesson.

DARE-TO-SERVE REFLECTION #36 *How could your personal purpose change the trajectory of your life?*

Nothing disturbs our soul like the idea of our life being without purpose . . . without impact . . . without meaning. Isn't that our greatest fear?

- That we won't be remembered?

- That our lives won't make a difference?

- That on the last day, we'll look around and say, "What was that all about?"

We quietly say to our souls, "Please do not let that be the case."

From 2001 to 2009, I encountered a series of life lessons. Nothing is more memorable than the lessons you learn the hard way. I was diagnosed with stage 1 breast cancer; fired from a job that I loved; had teenager challenges with our youngest child; and lost my mentor, my father.

Together these events led me to seek a deeper understanding of my personal purpose in leadership. I have decided to lead differently, to challenge myself daily to be more courageous and more humble. For the sake of others.

Don't wait for bad news to develop your convictions about leadership. Personal purpose transforms the focus, capability, and performance of the people.

Clarity of purpose will transform you, too.

EIGHT

AVOID THE **SPOTLIGHT**

THERE ARE A LOT OF THINGS IN LIFE that I know to be useful and true, but I still don't do them.

I know that keeping your life organized and orderly makes you more effective. But I don't care enough to act on it. I'm just not that bothered by messy desks and messy closets.

I know that budgets are useful planning tools, but I don't care enough to make a budget. For me, it's enough to know that there is still money in my bank account.

Similarly, you are reading about an approach to leadership that drives superior results, but you may not act on this information.

It all comes down to what you *believe* enough to act on. A belief is something so important to you that when it is violated, you are bothered to a point of distress. You become anxious, even angry. You want to act promptly to rectify the situation.

What beliefs do you care about so deeply that they shape your leadership actions?

My observation is that Dare-to-Serve Leaders act on these three core beliefs: human dignity, personal responsibility, and humility. In fact, when these beliefs are violated, the leader becomes distressed and quickly adjusts his or her behavior. These are difficult beliefs to teach leaders because they come from the soul.

Examining your soul, finding your deep-rooted beliefs, is the essential work of a leader. This is necessary preparation for serving others.

HUMAN DIGNITY

Without dignity, identity is erased.

LAURA HILLENBRAND, *UNBROKEN*

The stories of prisoners of war are both heartbreaking and inspiring. Our hearts break for the horrible things done to prisoners to defeat their dignity. And then we hear the story of a prisoner who was not defeated. Through intense focus, meditation or prayer, exercise, and communicating with other prisoners, the person's identity was intact. Their dignity survived. We are amazed at their story.

In these extraordinary circumstances, we can readily agree that every person deserves dignity.

Unfortunately, in the ordinary circumstances of the workplace, we are more careless with human dignity. We spend little time listening to our people. We are impatient with their imperfections. We expect them to listen to our problems and ideas, but express no interest in theirs. At the extreme, we humiliate; we publicly criticize and embarrass; we joke in ways that hurt.

Dare-to-Serve Leaders care deeply about protecting the dignity of people who work with them. This belief is evident in their daily actions.

They practice a simple rule, the Golden Rule: Do unto others what you would have them do unto you.

This one rule covers a host of circumstances. If you push your daily situations through a filter of what you would like someone to do for you, wouldn't you want to be listened to? Wouldn't you want the boss to be patient with your imperfections? Wouldn't you want them to take time to give you honest feedback and a clear development plan?

In a more difficult situation, where you are not performing up to expectations, wouldn't you want the Golden Rule to apply? Wouldn't you want to know where you stand?

DARE-TO-SERVE REFLECTION #37 *Have you committed to treating every person you lead with dignity, even in difficult circumstances? Could the Golden Rule become a core measure of your effectiveness?*

Every individual, including those having performance difficulties, deserves dignity. They deserve private conversations about the matter, away from public settings. They deserve thoughtful, specific examples to help them understand. They deserve time to absorb the feedback and time to work on personal improvement. If it becomes clear that they cannot stay in the job, they deserve help in understanding what strengths they have that will serve them well in another role.

Most leaders claim to value human dignity; far too many discard it quickly when under pressure at work.

Leaders who are stuck in the spotlight may even ignore or demean other people as a perverse way of keeping the attention on themselves.

Alternatively, if you apply the Golden Rule and treat others as you would want to be treated, you will take yourself out of the spotlight, and better serve your team.

Dare-to-Serve Leaders see each individual as a unique and valuable human being, worthy of dignity. And they treat them accordingly.

PERSONAL RESPONSIBILITY

A feature of man's maturity is
responsibility towards other people . . .
DIETRICH BONHOEFFER

In developing Dare-to-Serve Leaders, I have witnessed another stumbling block—the absence of personal responsibility. If people believe they have been a victim in this life or if they have a propensity to blame others for their problems, they will struggle to serve others well. It's as if "others" are not even on their radar.

You have witnessed this dichotomy in real life. Two children grow up in the home of a "deadbeat" parent. One child vows to change the course of his life and becomes an effective business and community leader with a healthy marriage and well-adjusted children. But the second child repeats history, becoming another "deadbeat" parent. What is the difference between the two people? Taking personal responsibility for their circumstances. Thinking about others, not just themselves.

This pattern exists among leaders. Some take ownership of their leadership and work to become better for the benefit of others. Some never accept responsibility and remain stuck in the spotlight.

Lack of personal responsibility in a leader is just another form of self-absorption. Victim leaders revel in their difficulties and blame the rest of mankind for their troubles. By definition, this thinking blinds them to the fact that the people they serve also have troubles. Such leaders cannot serve others well until they assume personal responsibility for improving themselves and develop empathy for others.

And so it is with Dare-to-Serve Leadership: to serve others well, you must look in the mirror—to see your own shortcomings and make the requisite changes in yourself. It is your personal responsibility to do so. You will have no capacity to serve others unless you can take responsibility for your own self.

My dad told me in my high school years, "After the age of eighteen, you are responsible for your own therapy charges."

Dare-to-Serve Leaders accept personal responsibility to improve themselves. They look in the mirror daily. They come to understand their own imperfections and this builds empathy for others.

There is a good tool for keeping yourself honest on this point. It is called the Accountability Ladder, and it was developed by the consulting firm Senn Delaney. It is a structured method for shifting your mindset from that of an unaware victim to a person accepting full responsibility for the next steps.

The way it works? You start at the bottom of the

Accountability Ladder

POWERFUL

Get on with it

Find solutions

"Own it"

Acknowledge reality

Wait and hope

Excuses

Blame others

Unaware

POWERLESS

Source: Senn Delaney.

"ladder" and talk yourself out of blame/victim status. Here is an example of how you use the Accountability Ladder, working your way from the bottom to the top:

My childhood home was completely dysfunctional (unaware).

My parents should have been better parents (blame others).

If they had been, I would be more successful (excuses).

That is why I am not getting promoted at work (wait and hope).

But I noticed this other person from the same background was recently promoted (acknowledge reality).

Perhaps, if I worked on improving my relationships with others, I would be promoted ("own it").

I'm going to ask a few of my closest colleagues for advice on improving relationships (find solutions).

Instead of worrying about getting promoted, I'm going to focus on having better relationships at work. That will improve my results and eventually result in more responsibility (get on with it).

Using the Accountability Ladder, this person has moved from being a powerless victim of circumstances to being a person who owns and acts on opportunities.

A leader without personal responsibility remains stuck in the spotlight and fails to serve others well. Dare-to-Serve Leaders, however, can't serve others until they have looked at themselves in the mirror, owned their circumstances, and accepted personal responsibility for pursuing solutions or opportunities.

DARE-TO-SERVE REFLECTION #38 *Where do you fall on the accountability ladder? What are you doing to assume personal responsibility for improving yourself as a leader?*

HUMILITY

Humility is not thinking less of yourself;
it is thinking of yourself less.

RICK WARREN, *THE PURPOSE DRIVEN LIFE*

I was once being interviewed for a leadership job in a restaurant company. The interviewer, a senior executive at the company, asked me about my approach to leadership. I said that I developed teams of highly competent people with their ego in check because I believed humility in leaders led to better teamwork and better performance. The executive actually leaped out of his chair and said, "That will never work here." Needless to say, I didn't get the job.

In sharp contrast, I remember one of my bosses explaining to me how profoundly he had been impacted by a chapter in *Mere Christianity*, by C. S. Lewis. The chapter title: "The Great Sin." The topic: Pride.

I went home that night and read the chapter. Over time, I have come to understand that self-centered pride resides in each and every one of us. Humility doesn't come naturally to anyone.

Our self-centered nature can be seen in a two-year-old child in the checkout line at the grocery store, lying flat out on the floor, screaming at the top of her lungs, fists clenched because Mom wouldn't buy her a candy bar. The child did not get what she wanted. A temper tantrum followed.

As adults, we have an inner two-year-old. We know what we want, when we want it, and we are despondent, annoyed, and even angry when we don't get our way. It's not appropriate to lie on the floor and scream anymore—but often, we are tempted.

True humility is not a destination we are likely to reach in life—but I believe great leaders aspire to be more humble. Humility is not being a doormat, it is simply thinking less about our own needs—and more about the needs of others. When we do this, we exit the spotlight, allowing us to serve others well.

The Dare-to-Serve Leader values humility, but admits that it is a struggle to be humble. As C.S. Lewis commented, "I wish I had got a bit further with humility myself."

I share his view. I am terrible at humility most days. But I know this to be true: followers appreciate humble leaders—leaders with the ability to admit mistakes, to apologize, and to be vulnerable in difficult circumstances; leaders who think of others more than themselves.

DARE-TO-SERVE REFLECTION #39 *Think of a humble leader whom you deeply admire. What qualities do you see in this person that you want to be evident in your leadership?*

Avoid getting stuck in the spotlight. Consciously move yourself outside the light, and see the difference it makes in how you serve others.

Early in my career, I attended a two-day workshop on time management skills. When I called home that night, the phone was answered by my three-year-old daughter, Katy. For some reason, I began excitedly sharing with her the things I had learned that day that I thought would forever change my life.

Katy listened to my thoughts and then responded by sharing the highlight of her day, "Mommy, today I learned this verse at vacation bible school: 'Now that you *know* these things, you'll be blessed if you *do* them.'"

Katy's words ring daily in my ears.

Step out of the spotlight. Focus on human dignity, personal responsibility, and humility, which are the essential beliefs for serving others well. Knowing these things is one thing. Doing them is far more difficult.

Choose the Dare-to-Serve path and be blessed.

CALL TO ACTION

Leaders are made by other leaders, and are made better by other leaders, and go on to make yet more leaders.

ALBERT MOHLER,
THE CONVICTION TO LEAD

WHEN YOU THINK OF LEAVING the leadership spotlight, do you get an anxious feeling in your stomach? Do you worry that you might miss out on fame or fortune? Do you fear you might become one of those "nice guys who finish last"?

As a leader, the most ambitious thing you will ever attempt is removing yourself from the spotlight.

It's harder than bungee jumping.

It takes all the bravery you can muster.

It knocks you onto your knees on a regular basis.

Dare-to-Serve Leadership is an extreme sport. It demands courage—and, in return, offers humility.

The Dare-to-Serve Leader has the *courage* to take the people to a daring destination and the *humility* to serve them well on the journey. The dynamic tension between daring and serving creates the conditions for superior results.

This is not for the faint-hearted.

Ponder this . . .

You've been given the role of leader. With that role comes tremendous influence and responsibility.

The people in your care are waiting, hoping, and praying that you will be a great leader.

Will they be disappointed or delighted when they reflect on your leadership?

THE INFLUENCE OF LEADERSHIP

The true measure of leadership is influence;
nothing more, nothing less.

JOHN MAXWELL

Today began with a phone conversation with a good friend, a mentor and a counselor. He said to me, "Cheryl, have you considered your influence?"

In my mind, I was thinking, "No, not yet this morning. I am still on my first cup of coffee."

Then he said, "Take the number of employees who work for Popeyes and multiply that by the number of hours in a workweek—and then by the number of weeks in the year."

Head spinning now. Definitely need more coffee.

"You have more influence than you know. Are you using that influence for good?"

Think about the math:

If you have 5 full-time people looking to you for leadership, in the year ahead, you have 10,000 hours of influence. You will likely spend more time with those five people than their parents, spouse, teacher, neighbors, or kids.

If you have 50 full-time people looking to you for leadership, in the year ahead you have 100,000 hours of influence.

DARE-TO-SERVE REFLECTION #40 *How will you use the opportunity for influence that you have been given? Will you dare to serve?*

If you have 500 full-time people looking to you for leadership, in the year ahead you have 1,000,000 hours of influence.

My friend is so right. Every leader has exponential opportunity for influence.

THE STEWARDSHIP OF LEADERSHIP

Business leaders are increasingly the stewards of civilization.

DR. MAX L. STACKHOUSE, *ON MORAL BUSINESS*

In his book *On Moral Business*, Dr. Stackhouse explains that traditionally the world's institutions—such as government, family, education, religion—have been forces for good. What if that role of being stewards of civilization now falls to business leaders? Will we be up to the task?

Business has a prominent role in the world today, driving economic growth in developing nations and teaching future leaders life and work skills. With this opportunity for influence comes a moral imperative to steward the people and the organization well.

Stewarding the future leaders of the world is a significant responsibility.

Think of the leader's role at the most basic level. At Popeyes, many of our restaurants are mini–United Nations, melting pots of ethnicities and cultures, working together behind the counter. In the larger world, the countries these people represent are sometimes at war with one another—but not in the restaurant, where they will thrive if their leader serves them well.

Your leadership actions will change lives for the better, leave them unchanged, or, regrettably, leave them worse off.

Which will it be?

You have some important decisions to make.

- Will you humbly serve others over your own self-interest?

- Will you pursue a daring destination for the people?

- Will you help others find meaning and purpose at work?

- Will you teach others the guiding principles of serving others well?

In the world today, this kind of leader is in short supply. This is evidenced by the lackluster performance results of many organizations and institutions.

There are not enough Dare-to-Serve Leaders to run global businesses. There are not enough Dare-to-Serve Leaders to create and operate small businesses. There are not enough Dare-to-Serve Leaders to run other institutions, such as government, education, the arts, and charitable organizations.

If there were, the global economy would be growing at an incredible pace. The world's problems would find solutions. The people would be well served. The performance results would be stunning.

The world needs you to become a Dare-to-Serve Leader. And then teach others the same lessons.

I could not be more excited to leave the future in your hands.

Remember, I am the optimist. I believe you will choose to influence and steward the people and the organization well. I believe you will step out of the spotlight and dare to serve.

I wish you great courage and deep humility.

And I promise you this, if you take action on what you have learned, you'll be blessed.

And so will those who follow you . . . for generations to come.

Dare-to-Serve Reflections

Part One: How to Drive Superior Results

CHAPTER ONE: Whom will we serve?

#1 *How do you think about the people you lead? Are they a "pain in the neck" or essential to the future success of the organization?*

#2 *Think about difficult leaders you have worked for. Have you made a conscious decision to lead differently than "them"?*

#3 *Who are the most important people you serve— the owner, the boss, the customer, the employees? Which one is your primary focus?*

#4 *What are the specific qualities you love in the people you lead?*

#5 *How do you gain meaningful feedback from those you serve?*

CHAPTER TWO: What is the daring destination?

#6 *What daring destination have you established for your team and organization? What strategies will ensure the team reaches the destination?*

#7 *What are the few vital things that must be addressed in your organization to drive better performance?*

#8 *Have you committed the resources needed to reach the daring destination?*

#9 *What steps have you taken to create a work environment that brings out the best performance from your team?*

#10 *What are the milestones and measurements of progress in your organization? Are you acting on what you learn from the data?*

CHAPTER THREE: Why do we do this work?

#11 *How well do you know the people who work for you? Do you know the three or four events of their lives that have shaped who they are today?*

#12 *If you knew the top-priority values of the people on your team, how would you lead more effectively?*

#13 *Most leaders can tell you the weaknesses of their team members. But can you cite the strengths and talents of your team? Are you accessing their very best capability?*

#14 *What would happen if you helped your team discover and pursue their personal purpose? How would they contribute differently to the performance of the team?*

CHAPTER FOUR: How will we work together?

#15 *What are the principles of your organization? Are they evident in the daily actions of the team members?*

#16 *How is passion demonstrated in the daily actions of you and your team?*

#17 *Are you and your team listening carefully and learning continuously from the people you serve?*

#18 *What process do you have for collecting and analyzing the facts? What process do you have for planning the future?*

#19 *What is your coaching routine? Do you have a specific and thoughtful development plan for each of your team members?*

#20 *How do you hold your team accountable and discourage victim mindsets or blaming others? How does your team hold you personally accountable?*

#21 *How do you and your team model humility in your daily actions?*

Part Two: How to Become a Dare-to-Serve Leader

CHAPTER FIVE: Choose to Serve

#22 *Who was your best boss? Who was your worst boss? Which one led you to your best performance results? Why?*

#23 *How would your daily behaviors be different if you put them through a filter of serving others well?*

#24 *How do you use the power that comes with your position: for personal gain or for serving the people and the enterprise?*

#25 *What is the most important achievement of your life? Was the win for you—or for the people on your team?*

#26 *Do you have big ambitions for yourself or big aspirations for the people on your team?*

CHAPTER SIX: Be Bold and Brave

#27 *How will your daring aspiration for the organization grow the capability and experience of the team?*

#28 *Think about a bold initiative that you have been a part of. How did it prepare you well for future leadership?*

#29 *What prevents you from pursuing a daring aspiration for the organization? Do you worry that others may think the plan is crazy? Do you have anxiety that you might fail?*

#30 *What is your daring aspiration for your team that is beyond what they know how to accomplish today?*

CHAPTER SEVEN: Have Clarity of Purpose

#31 *Why do you work? Do you have a purpose beyond paying the bills?*

#32 *Looking back over your life, what themes reoccur? How can you use those experiences to positively impact your team?*

#33 *How will your top-priority values contribute to the performance of your team and organization? How do you want to be remembered?*

#34 *What are your best talents that you can offer to the organization? Are you using those talents in your current role?*

#35 *When will you set aside time to reach clarity about your personal purpose for serving others?*

#36 *How could your personal purpose change the trajectory of your life?*

CHAPTER EIGHT: Avoid the Spotlight

#37 *Have you committed to treating every person you lead with dignity, even in difficult circumstances? Could the Golden Rule become a core measure of your effectiveness?*

#38 *Where do you fall on the accountability ladder? What are you doing to assume personal responsibility for improving yourself as a leader?*

#39 *Think of a humble leader whom you deeply admire. What qualities do you see in this person that you want to be evident in your leadership?*

Call to Action

#40 *How will you use the opportunity for influence that you have been given? Will you dare to serve?*

Notes

The Dare-to-Serve Leader

3 *There's nothing fundamentally wrong* . . . Robert Townsend, *Up the Organization* (New York: Knopf, 1970), 91.

6 *paradoxical mix* . . . James C. Collins, *Good to Great: Why Some Companies Make the Leap—and Others Don't* (New York: Harper Business, 2001), 39.

7 *Leadership Is an Art* . . . See Max De Pree, *Leadership Is an Art* (New York: Doubleday, 1989; reprint, New York: Crown Business, 2004); C. William Pollard, *The Soul of the Firm*, 1st ed. (Zondervan, 1996); and Rajendra S. Sisodia, Jagdish N. Sheth, and David B. Wolfe, *Firms of Endearment: How World-Class Companies Profit from Passion and Purpose*, 2nd ed. (Pearson Education, FT Press, 2014).

PART ONE: HOW TO DRIVE SUPERIOR RESULTS

Chapter One: Whom will we serve?

15 *It begins with the natural feeling* . . . Robert K. Greenleaf, *The Servant as Leader* (Robert K. Greenleaf Center for Servant Leadership, 2008), 15.

15 *your attitude is your altitude* . . . A similar quote to "Your

attitude is your altitude" is attributed to Zig Ziglar:
"Your attitude, not your aptitude, will determine your altitude."
The Ziglar Official Quote Library, http://www.ziglar
.com/quotes.

17 *Leadership Is an Art* . . . Max De Pree, *Leadership Is an Art* (New York: Doubleday, 1989; reprint, New York: Crown Business, 2004).

22 *Domino's franchisees sued the company* . . . Louise Kramer, "Franchisee Group Hits Domino's with Antitrust Suit," *Nations Restaurant News* 29, no. 36 (September 11, 1995): 7.

22 *long history of conflict* . . . Bill Carlino, "KFC, Franchisees Settle Lawsuit, Agree to End Bitter 7-Year Feud," *Nations Restaurant News* 30, no. 8 (February 19, 1996): 1.

22 *troubled franchisee/franchisor relationships* . . . Richard Gibson, "Have It Whose Way? At Burger King, Management and Franchisees Are Locked in Battle over the Company's Direction," *Wall Street Journal*, May 17, 2010; accessed on September 21, 2014, at http://online.wsj.com/articles/SB100014240527487048 69304575109240807702512. Jason Daley, "Why These 3 Once Thriving Franchises Have Fallen on Hard Times," *Entrepreneur*, August 4, 2014; accessed September 21, 2014, at http://entrepreneur.com/article/235379.

Chapter Two: What is the daring destination?

35 *The bravest* . . . Bayard Joseph Taylor, "The Song of the Camp," in *An American Anthology, 1787–1900*, edited by Edmund Clarence Stedman (Boston: Houghton Mifflin, 1900).

35 *paradox* . . . "Paradox," Merriam-Webster.com; accessed September 17, 2014, at http://www.merriam -webster.com/dictionary/paradox.

35 *oxymoron* . . . "Definition and Examples of Oxymorons"; accessed September 17, 2014, at http://grammar
.about.com/od/mo/g/oxymoronterm.htm.

38 *Would you tell me, please* . . . Lewis Carroll, *Alice's
Adventures in Wonderland* (Seahorse Classics, 2013),
chapter 6, 30.

41 *People think focus means saying* yes . . . Steve Jobs,
Apple Worldwide Developers Conference, May 13–16,
1997, quoted in George Beahm, ed., *I, Steve: Steve Jobs
in His Own Words* (Agate B2 Books, 2011), 43.

44 *Unless such commitment is made* . . . Peter F. Drucker,
Drucker Management: Tasks, Responsibilities, Practices (Allied
Publishers, 1974), 128.

48 *So much of what we call management* . . . Peter F. Drucker,
in Kevin Kruse, "100 Best Quotes in Leadership," Forbes
.com, October 16, 2012.

Chapter Three: Why do we do this work?

61 *Most of us* . . . Studs Terkel, *Working: People Talk about
What They Do All Day and How They Feel about What They
Do* (New Press, 2011), xi.

61 *one in ten Americans* . . . 2014 Restaurant Industry
Pocket Factbook, National Restaurant Association,
www.restaurant.org.

63 *State of the American Workplace* . . . Gallup, *State of the
American Workplace: Employee Engagement Insights for U.S.
Business Leaders*, 2013, www.gallup.com.

67 *[Work] is about a search* . . . Terkel, *Working*, xi.

68 *we use a deck of cards* . . . The John Maxwell Co.,
Leadership Values Cards, https://www.johnmaxwell
.com/store/products/Leadership-Values-Cards-%252d
-Qty.-12.html.

70 *we use an online assessment tool* . . . Marcus Buckingham,
StandOut, https://standout.tmbc.com.

Chapter Four: How will we work together?

81 *Alone we can do so little* . . . Joseph P. Lash, *Helen and Teacher: The Story of Helen Keller and Anne Sullivan Macy* (New York: Delta/Seymour Lawrence, 1981), 489.

82 *Why not just come right out* . . . James S. Kunen, "Enron's Vision (and Values) Thing," *The New York Times*, January 19, 2002; accessed September 21, 2014, at http://www.nytimes.com/2002/01/19/opinion /enron-s-vision-and-values-thing.html.

83 *Nothing great* . . . Ralph Waldo Emerson, *Essays: First Series—Circles* (1847).

86 *Don't assume* . . . Robert K. Greenleaf, *Servant Leadership: A Journey into the Nature of Legitimate Power and Greatness* (New York: Paulist Press, 1977), 314.

89 *There are abundant current examples* . . . Greenleaf, *Servant Leadership*, 40.

91 *To put it simply and starkly* . . . Larry Bossidy and Ram Charan with Charles Burck, *Execution: The Discipline of Getting Things Done* (New York: Crown Business, 2002), 141.

93 *The price of greatness* . . . Winston Churchill, "The Price of Greatness," speech given at Harvard University, 1943, www.winstonchurchill.org.

94 *Ego can't sleep* . . . Stephen Covey, foreword to Robert K. Greenleaf, *Servant Leadership: A Journey into the Nature of Legitimate Power and Greatness*, 25th anniversary ed. (Paulist Press, 2002), 7.

PART TWO: HOW TO BECOME A DARE-TO-SERVE LEADER

101 *Everyone thinks* . . . Leo Tolstoy, "Three Methods of Reform," in *Pamphlets: Translated from the Russian*, translated by Aylmer Maude (1900), 29.

Chapter Five: Choose to Serve

103 *Do nothing from selfish ambition* . . . Philippians 2:3,
The Holy Bible, English Standard Version.

104 *I've never known a person* . . . Jack Welch, *Winning*,
1st ed. (Harper Business, 2005), chapter 18.

107 *Greenleaf concluded* . . . Robert K. Greenleaf, *Servant
Leadership: A Journey into the Nature of Legitimate Power
and Greatness*, 25th anniversary ed. (Paulist Press, 2002),
21–61.

112 *Ambition is a cultural norm* . . . "Ambition," 1a,
Merriam-Webster.com; accessed September 17, 2014,
at http://www.merriam-webster.com/dictionary
/ambition.

113 *The definition of aspiration* . . . "Aspiration," 3a,
Merriam-Webster.com; accessed September 17, 2014,
at http://www.merriam-webster.com/dictionary
/aspiration.

Chapter Six: Be Bold and Brave

115 *I learned that courage* . . . Jessica Durando, "15 of Nelson
Mandela's Best Quotes," *USA Today*, December 6, 2013;
accessed September 20, 2014, at http://www.usatoday
.com/story/news/nation-now/2013/12/05/nelson
-mandela-quotes/3775255.

116 *Eric Brymer and Lindsay Oades* . . . Eric Brymer
and Lindsay G. Oades, "Extreme Sports: A Positive
Transformation in Courage and Humility," *Journal of
Humanistic Psychology* 49 (2009): 114–126.

Chapter Seven: Have Clarity of Purpose

131 *a deck of cards* . . . The John Maxwell Co., Leadership
Values Cards, https://www.johnmaxwell.com/store/
products/Leadership-Values-Cards-%252d-Qty.-12.html.

132 *Now, Discover Your Strengths . . .* Marcus Buckingham
and Donald O. Clifton, *Now, Discover Your Strengths*
(The Free Press, 2001).

133 *StrengthsFinder and StandOut . . .* See Marcus Buckingham, StandOut, https://standout.tmbc.com; and
the Gallup StrengthsFinder Assessment, https://www
.gallupstrengthscenter.com.

136 *It's not about you.* Rick Warren, *The Purpose Driven
Life* (Zondervan, 2002), 17.

Chapter Eight: Avoid the Spotlight

142 *Without dignity . . .* Laura Hillenbrand, *Unbroken: A
World War II Story of Survival, Resilience and Redemption*
(Random House, 2010), 183.

144 *A feature of man's maturity . . .* Eric Metaxas, *Bonhoeffer:
Pastor, Martyr, Prophet, Spy* (Thomas Nelson, 2010), 141.

145 *The Accountability Ladder . . .* Developed by Senn
Delaney. Larry E. Senn and John R. Childress, *The Secret
of a Winning Culture: Building High-Performance Teams*,
1st ed. (Leadership Press, 1999), 103.

148 *Humility is not thinking less . . .* Rick Warren, *The
Purpose Driven Life* (Zondervan, 2002), 148.

149 *I wish I had got a bit further . . .* C. S. Lewis, *Mere
Christianity* (C. S. Lewis Pte. Ltd., 1952, 1980), 128.

150 *Now that you know . . .* John 13:17, The Holy Bible,
New International Version.

Call to Action

151 *Leaders are made . . .* Albert Mohler, *The Conviction to
Lead: 25 Principles for Leadership That Matters* (Bethany
House Publishers, 2012), 14.

152 *The true measure of leadership . . .* John C. Maxwell,
The 21 Most Powerful Minutes in a Leader's Day (Thomas
Nelson, 2000).

153 *Business leaders . . .*   Max L. Stackhouse, Dennis P. McCann, and Shirley J. Roels, eds., with Preston Williams, *On Moral Business: Classical and Contemporary Resources for Ethics in Economic Life* (William B. Eerdmans Publishing Company, 1995), 12.

Acknowledgments

This book would not have made it into print without the love, encouragement, competence, and support of many people. I am indebted to all those who said an encouraging word, who offered help, who provided feedback, and who brought their own gifts and talents to this process:

To my husband, Chris, for his incredible patience with me during the year that it took to write and publish this book.

To Dr. Robert Thomas, faculty member at the Georgia Institute of Technology, for encouraging me to write this book and for introducing me to Berrett-Koehler Publishers.

To Steve Piersanti, president of Berrett-Koehler, for seeing a place for this book in the marketplace and for giving me the benefit of his wise counsel.

To Mark Levy, book writing coach and magician, for the dynamic way he taught me how to write.

To Bob Berry, for his design talent.

To Daniel Watts, my research assistant, and Donna Wilson, my executive assistant, for keeping the project and me on track.

To the servant leaders who have inspired me—Colleen Barrett, Art Barter, Ken Blanchard, Max De Pree, Phyllis Hendry, William Pollard, and Andy Stanley.

To the leaders whom I have learned from over the years—Emil Brolick, Doug Conant, Bill Connell, John Cranor, Laurel Cutler, Joel Davis, Patrick Doyle, Louis V. Gerstner, Jr., Aylwin Lewis, Charmaine McClarie, Tom Monaghan, Bob Murray, Denise Ramos, John Seeley, Sally Smith, and Dolph von Arx.

To author friends, who have shared their wisdom—Shaunti Feldhahn, Don M. Frick, Tim Irwin, Larry Julian, Scott MacLellan, Joel Manby, Lisa Earle McLeod, and James W. Sipe.

To the Popeyes board of directors, who supported my decision to write this book.

To the Popeyes Leadership Team for standing in the gap when I was consumed by the workload of job and book writing—I love you very much and deeply appreciate your support.

To the Popeyes franchise owners for being incredible partners in this turnaround story.

To friends and family, who reviewed draft titles, covers, and manuscripts.

To prayer warriors Mark and Debbie McGoldrick, Mac McQuiston, Dick Schultz, and Bob Tiede.

To Jesus Christ for his never-ending presence, love, and mercy.

I humbly and gratefully acknowledge that without all of you, this story could not have been told.

Index

About the Author

SCOTT HOUSLEY PHOTOGRAPHY

WHEN MY HUSBAND AND I went to my daughter's third-grade parent-teacher conference, the teacher looked at us and said rather sternly, "I don't know what Tracy is going to be when she grows up, but she is going to be in charge of it." At that moment, I had my first glimpse of what my mother's life must have been like. She raised four children and we all ended up in charge of something.

I've come to believe that our lives each have a theme, although sometimes it takes a long time to figure it out. At this point, I think it is safe to say that my life theme is leadership.

In the first chapter of my life, the theme was expressed by the *leaders in my family*—my grandparents and parents. I was blessed with family leaders who raised us in a safe, loving home, providing a good education, strong faith, and moral values. My father modeled the business leadership traits of competence and character in his career at National Semiconductor Corporation.

In the second chapter of my life, the theme was *learning* leadership—while serving as president of my campus sorority, Sigma Kappa, gaining my business school degrees at Indiana University, and apprenticing with strong leaders in brand management at Procter & Gamble and Gillette. I became fascinated with watching leaders, reading about leaders, and reflecting on leadership. I became a student of leadership.

The third chapter was about *being* a leader in large companies. I became a vice president at the young age of thirty-two and led marketing and product development teams at Nabisco and Domino's Pizza over the next dozen or so years. My career grand finale was supposed to be as president of KFC restaurants, a division of Yum! Brands. But instead, I learned some tough lessons—battling a round with breast cancer and an unsuccessful term as a restaurant company president. I experienced trials in leadership.

Yet another chapter spans the years of my marriage, from 1981 to the present day. My husband, Chris, and I are *co-leaders of our family*, raising three daughters with no manual other than the Bible. We've been imperfect parents, but we have loved the responsibility of leading our daughters to faith and to their own life theme.

As this book tells the story, the most recent chapter began when I was asked by the board of directors of Popeyes to lead a turnaround of this brand, famous for its Louisiana culinary heritage. This has been the best leadership opportunity of my life. With a supportive board, a capable team, a distinctive brand, and more than three hundred franchise owners invested for the long haul, we have been able to deliver a remarkable set of results. By doing so, we have established the business case for Dare-to-Serve Leadership.

I look forward to spending the rest of my days inspiring purpose-driven leaders who exhibit character and competence in all aspects of their lives. This is the calling of my life and I'm deeply grateful for the opportunity to serve.

WWW.DARETOSERVELEADERS.COM

Berrett–Koehler
Publishers

Berrett-Koehler is an independent publisher dedicated to an ambitious mission: *connecting people and ideas to create a world that works for all.*

We believe that to truly create a better world, action is needed at all levels—individual, organizational, and societal. At the individual level, our publications help people align their lives with their values and with their aspirations for a better world. At the organizational level, our publications promote progressive leadership and management practices, socially responsible approaches to business, and humane and effective organizations. At the societal level, our publications advance social and economic justice, shared prosperity, sustainability, and new solutions to national and global issues.

A major theme of our publications is "Opening Up New Space." Berrett-Koehler titles challenge conventional thinking, introduce new ideas, and foster positive change. Their common quest is changing the underlying beliefs, mindsets, institutions, and structures that keep generating the same cycles of problems, no matter who our leaders are or what improvement programs we adopt.

We strive to practice what we preach—to operate our publishing company in line with the ideas in our books. At the core of our approach is stewardship, which we define as a deep sense of responsibility to administer the company for the benefit of all of our "stakeholder" groups: authors, customers, employees, investors, service providers, and the communities and environment around us.

We are grateful to the thousands of readers, authors, and other friends of the company who consider themselves to be part of the "BK Community." We hope that you, too, will join us in our mission.

A BK Business Book

This book is part of our BK Business series. BK Business titles pioneer new and progressive leadership and management practices in all types of public, private, and nonprofit organizations. They promote socially responsible approaches to business, innovative organizational change methods, and more humane and effective organizations.

Berrett–Koehler
Publishers

Connecting people and ideas
to create a world that works for all

Dear Reader,

Thank you for picking up this book and joining our worldwide community of Berrett-Koehler readers. We share ideas that bring positive change into people's lives, organizations, and society.

To welcome you, we'd like to offer you a free e-book. You can pick from among twelve of our bestselling books by entering the promotional code **BKP92E** here: http://www.bkconnection.com/welcome.

When you claim your free e-book, we'll also send you a copy of our e-newsletter, the *BK Communiqué*. Although you're free to unsubscribe, there are many benefits to sticking around. In every issue of our newsletter you'll find

- A free e-book
- Tips from famous authors
- Discounts on spotlight titles
- Hilarious insider publishing news
- A chance to win a prize for answering a riddle

Best of all, our readers tell us, "Your newsletter is the only one I actually read." So claim your gift today, and please stay in touch!

Sincerely,

Charlotte Ashlock
Steward of the BK Website

Questions? Comments? Contact me at bkcommunity@bkpub.com.